Sept — Oct 2013.

Eastern,

enjc,

Mary.
x

STELLA DAYS

www.stelladays.ie
email: info@stelladays.ie

ISBN 978-1-907221-17-0

10 9 8 7 6 5 4 3 2 1

The paper used in this book comes from wood pulp of managed
forests. For every tree felled, at least one tree is planted, thereby
renewing natural resources.

A CIP catalogue record for this book is available from the British
Library.

STELLA DAYS

The Life and Times of a Rural Irish Cinema

MICHAEL DOORLEY

"I go down into the water
dive as deep as man can go
Into those dark places
watch the underwater flow;
Exploring the Blue
Exploring the Blue
Exploring the Blue
in search of you."

These words are from a song called 'Exploring the Blue', which I wrote in 1991. It is one of many songs in my life, which is drawn from the film world. *The Big Blue* is a Luc Besson film which tells the story of two boys in Sicily who's lifelong passion is to dive into the sea. It is a beautiful story; and one of those magical films which rendered me childlike before the screen, where I dive into this mysterious world, and experience the scenes before me. The cinema is the constructed dreamworld of every town and village in the world fortunate to have one. When my brother Christy took me to *The Great Escape* in the Odeon in Newbridge, Co. Kildare, I was Steve McQueen breaking out of prison, conquering the barbed wire on the motorbike. When the ads are over, and the lights go down, I enter the dreamworld, where I laugh, cry, am ecstatic, terrified, in other words, alive. The cinema is the only place where the world expands when the lights go out.

Cheers,
Barry.
LUKA BLOOM

Acknowledgements

With Sincere Thanks to True Friends:

Mary for being herself
Ruth, Joe & Maurice for their drawings
Philip for his patience
Luka for his kind words
AnnMarie for her music
Patrice for his bonhomme
Don for his advice
Diarmuid for his diligence
Brian for his prowess in print
Eamonn, Seanie & Paddy - there from the start
Jackie & Maggie for their courage and commitment

Thanks also to the National Library of Ireland
for research and reference.

CONTENTS

In the Beginning ...

'Borrisokane without a name,
A church without a steeple.
Cranky ould hoors,
Looking out half doors,
... criticising dacent people.'

– Anon

During Ireland's deep slumber of the 1950's, the town of Borrisokane presented a broadly similar appearance to today, that of a long street that had outlived the economic reasons for its existence and couldn't be less bothered. A small grey town, located at Munster's most northerly point, it is set amidst Tipperary's million green acres. Distinctly rural, its backdrop is an intricate patchwork of grasslands and tillage fields bounded by ditches, trees and patches of silent bog. These limestone lowlands are bordered by hills to the east and Shannon's Lough Derg to the west. They once formed the natural boundaries of the territory of Ely, fought over for centuries between two feudal warlords. The Gaelic O'Carroll clan and the Norman Butler dynasty eventually made peace through an arranged marriage and their descendants till the land to this day. Farming, both dairy and tillage, has always been the key activity in the area, generating a deep connection between the land and its people. The winding network of easy going roads, having faithfully followed the original cattle tracks, meander around every hill and hollow. Reliable signposts are scarce. On the road from Nenagh town, the traveller is greeted by a road sign inviting all to: 'Wine, Dine & Stay at the Yanks'. It's just a half mile to Borris. From here, the concrete water tower should be visible among the trees in the distance.

On entering the town, an elegant tree lined terrace of Georgian houses greets the visitor and seems to proclaim that one is not just entering a mere village. As with most small Irish towns, Borris ceased to grow by the end of the 19th century, giving it a sleepy timeless aura. Now with its slow rhythms, it appeared content with its status as a quiet backwater in an uncertain world. Like a prosperous farmer, the main street is wide, respectable and well proportioned. Although the tallish buildings are uniform, no two houses are completely alike. Rows of neat council cottages cluster along the side roads, each with a generous acre of back garden. No scarcity of land it would seem. The town had its own 'commons' constituting a vast prairie of some 30 acres of flat grassland with a walled-in hurling pitch at its centre. This was the epicentre, the sacred and hallowed turf graced by generations of athletes since time immemorial. It was owned by the Land Commission who received two shillings a year grazing rights from each of the owners of a retired plough horse, a piebald pony and seventeen bog-donkeys. This vast green expanse stretched as far as a child's eye could make out, before sloping down to the riverbank. From here the landscape blurred into deep marshes beyond the boundaries of lived experience. Parental advice revealed that this was 'the back of beyond', truly the Far Side.

The town of Borris, (always pronounced 'Burres', its original Norman name) was much more 'centred' then and was economically dependent on the farming population. Whilst the townspeople were mainly the families of shopkeepers, professionals and trades-people, the town owed its very existence to agriculture. It took its agrarian character, atmosphere and personality from the surrounding countryside. The farm holdings being well spread and isolated, the street was the common point of business and social contact for farming people. The land was not over generous and demanded much by way of labour. The farmers were sturdy, independent and hardworking but needed to come to town at least once a week. This was particularly evidenced by huge activity on fair and market days, when people and stock would flood into Borris from first light. They arrived for the day from a vast hinterland and the grocery shops, drapers and pubs all did brisk trade. The rural origins and ethos of the townspeople themselves were reflected in their seasonal activities, down to each household having a small patch of outlying bog or keeping an ass.

Weather was the dominant factor for both people and landscape. Being variable, it could range from hauntingly beautiful in summer, to morose in mid-winter. Each season cast its own spell on the landscape with dramatic light change a constant factor. Summers, although long and balmy in the memory, were rare and brief in reality. The timeless, verdant beauty of the Tipperary countryside manifests itself only in the most fleeting of glimpses. It may be just a hushed pause, but there is that magical moment, when the horizontal rays of the sun embrace the entire grey-green landscape and all is briefly well with the world. To linger on Carney Commons at sunset, watching for a wily hare or pheasant to break cover or listen to the territorial concerto of the blackbird, could prove an energising and redeeming experience. Past and present fuse in dreamy abstraction. As the sun generously splashes out its rays, and the light grows more intense, the timeless moor seems to breathe alive, brooding but beautiful. The greenery ignites in a riot of light and colour. Delicate wisps of bog cotton, purple orchids and yellow birds-foot would reach upwards in glimmering response. Rank growth, having thus gripped the countryside, now attempted to engulf the town. With speed and stealth, ivy snaked up dank walls and scutch-grass surged through every crevice. Weeds, such as thistle and ragwort, would blossom in the most ludicrous locations. Briars, nettles and moss covered rocks would obstruct all but the best trodden paths. The old corn mill with its ancient limestone walls and windows rendered in faded yellow brick was colonised each summer by wildlife of every description. The swallows arrived to annex the top floor making their noisy forays down and across the river. The starlings ruled the mid regions, leaving the ground floor as disputed territory – a virtual combat zone between rats, mice and Heenan's cats. Dark green weeds would clog the timeless flow of the river, now reduced to a mere rivulet. Nature was ready to reclaim its dominion at the first sign of dereliction in any wall or building.

Summer would gradually fade into autumn, leaving a marked change of mood and temperature, under the Atlantic clouds. The light changed from the rich hues of an oil painting to the pastel shades a misty water-colour. The woods shrouded themselves in gorgeous colours of yellow and brown in the manner of a Constable or Turner landscape. The Shi-Gaoith (Fairy Wind) blew dead leaves in a magic circle around the school-yard, before depositing them in a pile against the back door. The swifts, house-martins and swallows had defected at the first drop in temperature. The hardy council workers fulfilled their seasonal task of weeding the river, leaving odd heaps to dry on the river bank.

Come winter, the land would sink to a sullen waterlogged grey. It rarely snowed, but when it did, the world came to a virtual standstill. Nature might happily connive to freeze the school pipes, granting the children freedom from the tyranny of the classroom. It was child's-play now to track the unsettled Arctic hare, meandering against a white background. The thaw came all too soon. Rain and damp were pervasive. A howling malevolent east wind, fit to whip warts off a bullock, would rage along the Main Street where by times rolling tumbleweed would not have seemed out of place. People stayed indoors for fear of murderous slates flying from the roofs of old buildings. Amongst the older folk, there was awesome respect for the ultimate power of nature and this was most evident in the deepest days of winter. The combination of minimal street lighting and shorter daylight hours wrought a potent fusion between imagination and darkness. In November (the month of the holy souls), a child would gaze in awe at the 17th century Church of Ireland and its adjoining graveyard. This was home to the town's colony of bats. The twilight created its own illusions. Tall leaning tombstones, standing at odd angles against the darkening backdrop of a winter sky, lent a gothic supernatural dimension. Extra sensory perception was not required to see, feel and hear the ghostly souls of the dead returning to their graves for another year, after a month of pagan revelry. On scurrying home, one could listen up through the chimney, to hear the howling of demon dogs in the distance and know that bed was the safest option that night. Reports would filter in from the country of fallen trees, isolated herds and stricken telegraph poles blocking the roads. The river, a mere brook during the summer, now turned to a raging torrent in a headlong rush to the broad waters of the river Shannon.

The town always had a vague midway feel about it, equidistant as it was between the larger Midland centres of Nenagh, Portumna and Birr. Probably by virtue of its location and relative isolation, Borris had its own distinct rhythms and time honoured way of life. Lifestyle was regulated by the demands of agricultural life which was seasonal and church life which was regular. This unhurried pattern was complimented by the clockwork rhythms of school and small time commerce. It was a world dominated by the common currency of conversation more than any urgent need to keep the wheels of industry rolling. But its soul lingered in the agrarian past, while slow-time waltzing with a humdrum present, with little thought for a vague future.

An emigrant returning in 1957, after even 20 or 30 years abroad, would have no bother recognising the town, so little had changed. A bit less dust rising from the street, now that it had been garnished with its first coat of tar and gravel. Hopping off the bus, a blast of native air would momentarily go to the head, intoxicating like vintage wine. Weary exile eyes would scan the street, looking for both familiarity and change. The wide tapering Main Street would have looked much the same, its neat rows of wooden shop-fronts punctuated by stone arches and narrow lane-ways. The mix of familiar names over the shop doors, such as Hough, Heenan, Kent, D'arcy, Seymour, Cleary, Cahalan, Moore, Egan and Crawford, each reflected the ancient fusion of Hiberno, Norman and Anglo forebears. The only trace of the long gone ascendancy (the Tower, Stoney and Nash families) were the side streets named for them. The huge lime tree overhanging the convent school wall was a dominant feature in the centre of the street. Old Phil's decommissioned Land Marshall tractor stood static in the square since time immemorial and didn't look like it would be mobile or active any time soon. The sleepy Square, set out in the manner of an Italian piazza, gave pride of place to an elevated iron fountain spouting a torrent of spring water. This was the main source of the town's drinking water and head-scarfed ladies bearing white enamel buckets would linger for chat as part of their daily routine. Appropriately, the moulded head of a bearded man on the fountain, water gushing from his mouth, was Hercules and he was looking towards the bridge. The mythical connection between Hercules and water occurs in the Roman epics. We are told that as he was still brooding over his choice between Virtue and Pleasure, he had looked towards river when: 'Seized by a thirst he scooped up the earth, caused Scamander the underground river god to burst forth.' The narrow stone bridge spanning three arches had presided for centuries over the lazy Ballyfinboy river. No Danube this, a small river by any standards, running at very low ebb in the summertime. But enough water, it seemed. Enough indeed to motivate the Quakers to build a corn mill there in the late 18th century, which by the 19th century had grown to become a major employer. Enough water to be harnessed by the enterprising Brereton family to generate their own electricity in the early part of the 20th century. And more than enough to keep a whole crop of youngsters occupied, swimming, fishing and poaching for that glorious span of their childhood between infancy and teens. The bridge end was still dominated by the mill with its mill-race, weir, pond and iron sluice gates. But the river dictated its own pace. Generations came, grew, lived, loved, grieved and went, but the plucky little river flowed on towards to the Shannon, ever indifferent to the past and whatever the future might hold.

ON MAIN STREET

'Memory is like a dog that lies down where it pleases'
— Cees Nooteboom

On the face of it, not a lot ever seemed to happen but herein lay its beauty. Nature rarely hurries. The focus fell on the inhabitants as they moved around their familiar orbit. Being a typical rural community, everyone knew the other by 'seed, breed and generation'. The pace of life could be best described as glacial. They had modest expectations and faced life with an odd mixture of wit and stoicism. Ruminate, they did not. They knew their lives were hard and the world does not always work out but they weren't reared to expect any different. Their's was a meagre self-sufficiency. Whilst they vaguely hoped for the best, instinctively they were ready for the worst.

Not that they dwelt too long on these matters. They certainly did not pursue self knowledge to the point of questioning whether their lives were fulfilled. They got on with it. They were highly engaging, humour and wit were their escape valves. A good belly-laugh was considered the best antidote to life's trials. Self-consciousness was considered a weakness but dialogue could be used to conceal or disguise in a subterranean linguistic code when dealing with strangers. The notion that life should be 'comfortable' or people be 'fulfilled' would have been a relatively obscure one. Any sign of taking oneself too seriously was in plain bad taste. There was also a curious detachment from material things (with the passionate exception of land ownership) and those qualities which are now considered vital to progress. The people were closely linked by bonds of blood, location, history and experience. Although conservative to the point of reactionary, there was a broad sense of decency and morality and the concept of fair play was considered very important. Socially acceptable behaviour was monitored at street level.

The main street was a wide and watchful street. Even when quiet, little happened there that did not become instant public knowledge. Personal crime, other than petty matters, was either non-existent or well concealed. It was often claimed that door latches outnumbered locks at that time. The main street was central to the life of the whole parish. This was where people met, where children played, fairs took place and life on the street was lived very much 'front of house'. But nothing was valued more than the art of good conversation and there was always a hunger for news. There were those who needed to hear it and those who just as badly needed to tell it. They had good retention, long memories and were grateful for any distraction to stop what they were doing and latch on to a chat with glee. That odd urban middle class concept of minding one's own business held little sway here and unflattering gossip was one of life's delights. There is an old Irish saying – 'Dúirt bhan liom, go dúirt ban lei' meaning – 'A woman told me, that a woman told her.' This beautifully sums up how a story can spin and grow. The topics could range from health to wealth, down to a cure for warts or a tip for a horse. The shopkeeper constantly sweeping the footpath outside of his little draper shop was generally doing so on a need-to-know basis rather than any obsession with street cleanliness. The bank porter polishing the brasses so meticulously on the doors of the bank could observe all the better the comings and goings of commercial and social traffic. It was inevitable that sometimes facts became secondary to stories. Good stories and in time, stories accrue meaning.

The only traffic hazard back then was likely to be the odd ponderous milk lorry or tractor, raising a trail of dust in its wake. Willie, who drove the oil lorry for Henderson & Bailey's Garage made sure he saluted everyone lest he be considered stand-offish. Not all rustic harmony though and life's realities would manifest themselves daily, as exemplified by the 'Burnhouse' lorry with its cargo of stinking carcasses wending its way up

Tower Hill. Every schoolchild on the street was on cue to dash indoors in an attempt to avoid the lingering smell. The gaunt Victorian workhouse overlooking the town was a stark reminder of times of past failure and destitution. The adjoining cemetery had just one headstone – for a hundred anonymous graves. Benefits, such as public health could not be taken for granted and the spectre of poverty still loomed, especially for large families. There was hardship also of the genteel variety, unseen behind closed doors. The devastating horrors of TB and polio had only finally abated in 1958. Life was tough for many people and the focus was on getting by. To survive and 'keep one's feet under the table' was enough for now, as prosperity was the loftier aspiration of those who would emigrate. But for those at home in a small tight knit community, there was the support structure, loyalty and empathy of good neighbours to ease life's burdens.

High fashion or modernity had little place on the agenda of daily living. In social terms alone, it was something of a man's world. Women did not smoke cigarettes or even whistle in the street as it would have been considered vulgar. Neither would they have taken a drink in a public bar as they were expected to occupy the more cloistered environs of the 'snug'. Perhaps a reflection of the times, clothing was dull in appearance and texture, forty shades of grey being a fair description. The working men wore peaked cloth caps in a manner that spoke of conformity as much as shelter. The caps were well worn to the point that they were moulded to the head, usually with the peak low over the eyes. It seemed the only time they were removed was when the Angelus bell rang. The cap would be taken off and grasped piously in both hands to the chest. The bald dome of a bowed head would appear, garnished with a few wisps of lank hair. At conclusion, the cap would be replaced and with a shuffle and a spit, the conversation would recommence. The hat was higher up on the social scale and indicated an occupation of some importance, such as that of a cattle jobber. Although some of the womenfolk sported colourful head-scarves, many of them in bereavement still wore a traditional black diamond on the sleeves of their overcoats. In the old European style, the more devout ladies wore mantillas in church. Fashion had just began to come into flavour late in the decade on the back of new fabrics made from nylon or Terylene and that icon of female conformity, the house-coat, would soon come into its own.

SHOP LOCAL

Self service shopping was unknown, so grocery shopping for the family was as socially important as it was necessary. There was a strong loyalty to those shopkeepers whose flexibility (in terms of credit) had helped many a poor family in the past. But now the shopkeeper and customer exchanged civil conversation and a dollop of gossip thrown in with the small change. In summer, the morning opening of the shop was itself a ritual. The wooden shutters were opened, allowing laser beams of sunlight to stream in through the glass and illuminate cosmic particles of dust inside. The external doors were then opened and the flagstone floors sprinkled with disinfectant and water, to keep down the dust. The pavement in front was swept clean. A special striped cloth was placed on the hall doors to protect the paint-work from peeling in the sun. A tiny bell over the door heralded the entrance of the day's first customer.

Children were expected to be 'seen but not heard' but were quick to learn the foibles of the adult population. They had a template for gauging the relative decency of a shopkeeper. The currency was ice-cream, served between wafers. One good woman used a knife to cut a threepenny or sixpenny ice-cream and always erred on the large side. The only snag was that the knife was often used to cut carrots or turnips beforehand, giving the ice-cream an unusual flavour. Conversely, the old man in the corner shop had a special plastic mould which was supplied by the conniving manufacturers. He would take ages measuring and cutting, agonising at the thought of his profit margins under threat. To smaller kids who hadn't travelled far and didn't possess much by way of pocket money, the shop window displays were alluring. Babe's had an array of biscuits and boiled sweets that seemed positively exotic in origin, gobstoppers being a speciality. Ernie, the saddler, operated from a little shop on Tower Hill that could only hold three people standing up. The grocer's window gave pride of place to the leading washing powders of the day, Surf, Omo and Daz. The shop reeked with the smell of carbolic soap. The chemist shop was more than a mere chemist shop. No, this building proudly proclaimed itself 'The Medical Hall' with Archibald G. Cooke MPSI in smaller letters underneath. The window held a contrasting display of toiletries such as Lifebuoy, Lux and Palmolive soaps, alongside Max Smile razor blades. Shoulder to shoulder with these luxuries were boxes of Cyrex Worm Drench and Armstrong's Liver Fluke Dosage alongside Sloan's Liniment with a picture of a patently healthy mustachioed Mr Sloan on the box. The aroma of whatever medical mix was being dispensed was sophistication itself. Inside was a regal weighing scales, which would function on the insertion of a single hen penny and displayed a capability of weighing up to 25 stone!

Lamb's window had the full range of sensible shoes with wellingtons in all sizes hanging from above. The finest of knicker elastic could be purchased at 3d a yard. Power's musty bookie office only came alive on big race days when the staff grew from one to three. But pride of place went to Lawlor's Christmas window display every year. The constant crowd of schoolchildren would stand six deep in a trance-like state craning for a view. Every conceivable toy, from the best in Meccano sets to the latest Cowboy hardware was set out against a backdrop of red crepe paper and coloured lights. The window was a temple of seasonal delights to be adored, a virtual bazaar of colourful toys. In frugal times, this was truly a window to a world of unimaginable possibility. Soon they would gather to witness a phenomenon which combined the colours of Christmas with the technical magic of cinema.

Being a conservative community, change or innovation was often greeted with scepticism. The most modern feature then would have been the black telegraph poles lined along each side of the street bringing an odd urban feel to a pastoral community. Rural electricity had arrived to a reluctant populace only in the previous decade. In some cases it had taken convincing that there was a viable future in household electricity supply. Old Mrs Conway, worrying that the 'electric' might burn her house down as she slept, finally conceded to having it installed on the basis that:

'Yer, It might come in handy ... for lighting the lamp.'

Certainly the telegraph poles played a salient role in the street-scape, be it for tethering the an ass or parking a bike. The telegraph wires were a god-send to the flocks of starlings and swallows who held pride of place as seasonal street spectators.

THE GOOD FOLK

'I love those dear hearts and gentle people',
who live in my home town'

- Bob Hilliard

Whilst the traditional values of hospitality, humour and humanity prevailed, identity was all important. Local nicknames were very popular. For example, men with the Christian name Michael were referred to as Brud. A man from Galway was known only as Killimor, the town he came from. There was Pat the Diamond, Gallons Hogan and Rootie Carroll. There were more colourful nicknames, which often highlighted some family feature and not always appreciated by the bearer. Although still bound in the outdated class structures of social position, there was genuine pride in individual identity. Ironically, there was something of a moral apathy to events in the world at large. It was a place where local community affairs took precedent over anything on the national stage. This was before the full impact of mass media, and communication was chiefly oral in all its nuances. The daily newspapers were read, particularly the *Irish Independent* with its front page taken up by the announcements of births, marriages and deaths. But the local paper, the weekly *Nenagh Guardian* was more popular. It was scrupulously dissected for information, the best bits being read out loud for everyone's benefit. The reports of minor misdemeanors from the court, fines for 'found-ons' in pubs or for no light on a bicycle, often made for hilarious reading. No stretch of the imagination was spared for excuses. Wednesday was the half-day in the town and with everywhere shut, one could not literally buy a box of matches. Sunday was special, the day when the 'servile' work of commerce and farming ceased in its entirety and the main street resembled a ghost town by afternoon. The silence could be deafening in its intensity. The only audible sign of life on some summer Sundays was the voice of match commentator Michael O'Hehir on radio. The sound would boom out to a deserted street through the rippling curtains of an open living room window. It was surreal. Not a soul in sight as all were inside listening to the big match on the wireless.

'A high dropping ball ... to the edge of the large parallelogram ... McKenna strikes ... it's a goal!'

The family dog asleep at the door, having been earlier ejected from the sitting room would open one lazy eye in muted response. A murder of crows would quarrel over a piece of stale bread in the convent yard. Beyond that, the town was in communal deep space. Local activities at that time would have been highlighted by posters in various shapes, sizes and states of decay on the large wooden door of the old Scout's Hall. A large faded yellow poster would have advertised the forthcoming attractions of Tom Duffy's – 'Ireland's Greatest Circus', which had rendered such a dazzling performance in Brereton's field – two years previously. A second poster advertised the annual Macra na Feirme field day, the bucolic highlight of which would be the ploughing match with some very attractive prizes. A great day out! First prize was an eight foot iron gate, second prize a leg of mutton and third prize 15lbs of Bellew's top grade grass seed. Between a notice advertising an auction for new meadow hay and a poster highlighting the illegality of ragwort was a small hand-written note inviting any parties interested in the setting up a community cinema to a meeting in the Legion Hall. It was only a possibility but something new was in the air, something to celebrate rather than question.

SOCIAL & ECONOMIC

'That money talks,
I'll not deny.
I heard it once.
It said....Goodbye!'
- Richard Larmour

In Ireland, it was towards the latter days of a period of economic stagnation that went back to the disastrous 'economic war' with Britain in the 1930s. It was indeed a grey old world. If ever a decade merited being portrayed in the medium of black and white film, this was it, truly the 'lost decade'. The striking parallels between Ireland of the 1950's and Ireland today is economic failure, wide scale despair at the multiple flaws of political leadership that brought a new republic to economic stalemate. The 1950's were likely the most economically depressed period in Ireland in the 20th Century. Emigration, that most profound and sustained experience of Irish history, was at its peak. It is estimated that three out of every four young people born in the 30s had emigrated by the 50s, such was the lack of opportunity for young people. Economically the year 1957 is regarded by many as the lowest point in the history of the State. Even people with jobs left by choice. Crucially, the population had fallen to under 3 million and the continuing decline gave coinage to the term 'the vanishing Irish'. It reached a crucial point where in common with only one other country in the world, Argentina, there were now more cattle than people on the land. In Borris, employment prospects were few and far between. The small quarries lay unworked, having yielded the best of stone over the years. The one guarantee of work for school leavers used to be Williamson's sawmills. But its main source, Borris Wood, had been depleted and was eventually levelled for a racecourse and the mills closed down. There was usually ample work with the farmers who concentrated on tillage and needed extra labour in the spring and summer. For a young person to be accepted into service in a pub or a doctors in the town was considered a good start. However, the wages and future prospects were meagre. In any event, on the switch to dairy produce following the establishment of the local creamery, the requirement for farm labour dried up. But people and quality of life cannot be measured in purely economic terms. The extremely conservative culture of the time had its repressive downside but it was a safer world for vulnerable older people. The statistics of the year reveal a social stability now confined to the realms of history. For example, a total of just seven murders were reported in the State in 1957 and these remained headline news for a long time. Luckily, the slump at home coincided with a postwar boom in England to where so many local people had migrated in search of work. In some cases, houses were abandoned completely as whole families left for England.

The only tourism then was the emigrant's annual return home for holidays. The official state response to the economic plight was 'let's party' and the 'An Tostal' festival was born. The event was sponsored by Bord Fáilte in an effort to woo emigrants and others to celebrate Ireland as a holiday destination. Every city, town and village had its 'Tostal Programme' and Borris was no exception. The colourful arrivals usually caused a bit of a stir in the town. One man who was so enthusiastic about the delights of life in the metropolis on the far side of the Irish sea, became known only as 'Lovely London', his real name forgotten. He had wondrous tales of red buses, black bobbies, and even underground trains. His only disappointment with London was despite several visits to Piccadilly Circus there was no 'Big-Top' – not even a clown to be seen! On his first visit back home he explained, in a cockney accent, how he had secured a good job 'laying the black stuff' for the 'North Tipp County Council' in Camden Town! After a week home, Borris was the best place again. It had the best people, best jokes, best pints and best spuds on the planet. But he would never settle back, as the prospects for his family were far better in London. Plenty of work.

Emigration apart, Borris was not a place you would pass through at high speed. If more than a dozen cars went through on a Sunday heading to a match somewhere, it was noted by the locals sitting on the 'bridge below the town' and considered worthy of mention in the Borrisokane notes in the *Nenagh Guardian* of the following week.

Fair Day

'It was a 'Pig Day' in November.
A day I'll ere remember....
As I walked the busy streets
in drunken pride.'

- Anon

Borris was described in our geography book in school as a 'small market town' and indeed the charter for the traditional market went back four centuries. The fairs were held every quarter, with the biggest of all fairs being held on 10th March. In later years a local man, Tom Kelly, added a few more to fill the gap between these dates and these became known as Kelly's fairs. Tom was a wonderful planner. His fairs were highly organised affairs, with the sheep confined to the bottom end, the cattle at the top and depending on the time of year, the turkeys or hens in the middle. It looked like organised chaos, an absolute orgy of sights, sounds and smells. It provided the opportunity for the local eccentrics to meet their counterparts from the surrounding districts. A huckster selling ropes of dubious origin, had the cheek to set up his pitch outside the finest hardware store in the town. The three card trick merchant known as Trick o' the Loop had to be fit and fast at turning a buck. He was ever ready to wind up his trestle table and disappear on first sight of the gardaí. Maggie May would never sell one of her hens on a wet day for fear of bad luck. She loved to tell the children about 'Louis', her pride and joy. Apparently Louis was a chicken who had been beheaded by some ghastly mistake. Maggie would excitedly point out the odd stitching around Louis's neck, where the head had been stitched back in place. Old Louis certainly played his part. But this story did not ring true, even to the most incredulous schoolchild. The odd thing was that as she told the story, the loose fold of flesh which hung from her own scrawny neck became strangely animated. The childish mind boggled and it was easier to consider Maggie herself as a much more likely candidate for a near-death or 'out of the body' experience. The shopkeepers had the inconvenience of having to place a makeshift barricade across their front doors to protect their premises. An overexcited heifer with haphazard bowel movement was not a welcome visitor in a draper shop. But the shopkeepers did not complain, as these were by far the busiest days of the year. The pubs and hotels did major trade and it was not unusual for the publican to hang up a little sign requesting the bargaining patrons to refrain from spitting on the floor. Noisiest day of all was 'Pig Day' when the excited squeals of young bonhams and old sows rent the air. There was great bustle and excitement surrounding the Fair Days, as it brought much business, movement and colour to the streets. The local council workers could vouch for this aspect, as they spent much of the evening and following day cleaning up the splashy residue of these colourful movements. At the weigh-yard towards evening the catch-cry would ring out

'One more for Conroy ... and the wagon is full.'

This was a signal that the trade was coming to a close and it was time to either go home or adjourn to the pub to spend the 'luck money'. At this call, the stragglers who featured at every fair would depart. First to go were the Drifters, the Drovers, the Herders, the Hoofers, the Jobbers, followed by the Tanglers, the Tinkers, the Hustlers, the Hucksters and the Rustlers, the Three-Card Trick Merchants, the Wheelers, the Dealers and lastly the Galway Sheep-stealers would all melt into the night. One inebriated mid-lands cattle dealer, who had earlier that day booked in to the Central Hotel, was seen to shuffle along a deserted street well into the wee late hours. As he floundered along, for support he gripped the silver railing alongside the Methodist church, like an exhausted mountaineer clutching his way to the summit. On arriving at the large dark portals of the old Victorian building, he proceeded to knock but got no reply. Panic, combined with the effects of an afternoon's frenzied trading set in and he started to bang loudly on the front door. The only other figure on the street was the portly sergeant with the stoat-like eyes, who had been taking an active interest in the stranger's movements.

'My good man, in the name of God what are you trying to do?'

'I p-paid a deposit and left my l-luggage in this hotel, Sergeant, you'd think the leasht they would do would be to let me in.'

'Not much chance of that tonight, my friend.'

'Why so?'

'That's the door of the National Bank you're trying to break down!'

Night Life

'The night has a thousand eyes
And the day but one'
— Francis Bourdillon

Such was the pace of life that it was rare to see anybody in too much of a hurry. Mag Griffin's hens seemed to spend most of their time pecking along the street and they were certainly not in much danger of being run over by passing traffic. Time was a generous commodity and seemed to stretch from the horizon to the sky, full of possibility. There was little to prevent the wanderer from going wherever they pleased. There were no trains or planes to catch and the bus from Nenagh trundled in once a week. The nearest railway station was Cloughjordan which could be reached by navigating over five miles of winding road. If that journey was to be made during the 'beet campaign' (harvesting season) then best to avoid the legions of men piking beet into wagons day and night. Many of the residents of the Main Street were odd and nocturnal in their habits. Given the complete absence of motor traffic – particularly after dark – people rarely seen in daylight would stand at their doorways at night chatting away to passers-by or hailing 'ice-breakers' to their neighbour directly across the street.

'Hey Yousorr, how's she cutting?'

'Ah ... fair to middling.'

'You'd notice the change in the hour, all the same.'

'I dunno, I think it's worse it's improving.'

With only dim street lighting at dusk, the faint luminous glow from a street light or a shop window would draw clandestine figures, sharing cigarettes and tall tales. The disembodied voices of these nocturnal natterers would echo into an endless night. On balmy summer evenings, the night air would echo backwards, forwards and across to the sound of doors opening and human voices coming up from the street. This would be punctuated by restless howls from McKenna's kennels in the Square. Twenty agitated greyhounds, driven to insomnia and distraction by the carry-on of Cleary's cats cavorting on top of the galvanized roof of the kennels. Some nights these sounds would merge alongside the shrieks of Horrigan's ferocious geese, who haunted the river day and night. It was considered unthinkable to raise children without the benefits of canine companionship, so most families kept a dog, usually fifth generation mongrels. The typical town dogs were small, the most common streak being a wiry class of terrier. The dogs on the street seemed part and parcel of the community, each having their niche in society, referred to as if human and indeed acknowledged for their individual personalities. 'Hitler' Houlihan was mad. A stir crazy black sheep-dog, with a white mane, he sat beside the street all day waiting to ambush cars. They were scarce but when one appeared, he would chase it down the street barking and snarling before halting at the bridge exhausted. He would then wait an hour or two for the next car which he could chase back up home. You would need to be careful of 'Lip' Heenan some days. While he had good nature in him, he could have a nasty temper when annoyed. 'Grouse' Carroll was a great dog for finding lost sliotars or bringing in saliva covered sods of turf but she was a terrible rambler. Her jaws were like vice-grips and she once dragged a heavy suitcase all the way up St Brigid's Avenue to home. Blue Meara was a rarely seen Kerry Blue. His existence could only be verified by poking a stick or hurl under its owner's back door and await the most vicious snarls imaginable. Sleeping most of the day on the footpath was the mange ridden 'Lucky' Byrne, with his three legs and one sad eye looking up at you, enough to frighten a pig. 'Scutter' Sullivan had worn out his welcome in the town's gardens and back lanes years previously and was far and away the most unwelcome member of the canine community. The town dogs lived long idle lives and were oftentimes as eccentric as their owners.

Apart from a Fair Day, Sunday was the 'busy' day with a crowd going to Mass in the morning and maybe a match in the afternoon. But talk about laid back. On Sunday mornings, one lady publican would take a glance at the clock, put on her hat and coat and head off to Church, leaving her five regulars to run the place in her absence. The conversation would drift on, punctuated only by the loud tick of the ancient pendulum clock. When the glasses gradually emptied, one of the customers would get up and slowly serve the drinks to the others. So it was 'business as usual' until the proprietor returned an hour or so later. Clearly a more innocent and easy going age.

Whilst economic stagnation and emigration were everyday acts, it was not a gloomy place. These were people who had coped with a lot in their time and had learned along the way how to manage, by laughing. The people were ordinary, hospitable and good humoured in the main. Stories based on hearsay were told, added to and repeated so often that some of them eventually became true. There were old codgers who claimed to know of ghosts and banshees and were only too happy to elaborate. At a deeper level there was a healthy respect for the unseen or spiritual dimension. Above all, there were men and women of wit and wisdom who loved to tell a good story to anyone who cared to listen. Independent, slow talkers with a droll sense of humour, they never seemed to take life too seriously. They always expected that somehow tomorrow would be better than today 'Please God' and chose to live in hope, rather than despair. There was an element of poetry in even the simplest things, as it was never a case of just 'Hello'. Some were undoubtedly eccentric. One would still have to be wary of prolonged conversation unless possessed of a speedy riposte to some of the questions posed as answers. Anyone with airs or pretensions were mercilessly exposed. These people's sharp wit was the product of tough economic times but it shaped the local view of the world. Certainly, for any would-be film screenwriter, there was a wealth of character material and unpredictable dialogue readily available. A working knowledge of the devious lore of Hiberno - English would be the key requirement. To children, all the world is truly a stage and ordinary everyday characters can take on imagined melodramatic qualities not apparent from an adult perspective. But were they ordinary characters? A keen listener, one who could discern between gems of wisdom and flights of whimsy could be rewarded with a lifetime's education in applied philosophy. It was also a time when old people were held in awe for their wisdom, given the obvious length of time they had been in the world. Essentially a storyteller had to be old to achieve any type of credibility. In terms of singularity and individuality, some wry examples immediately spring to mind.

Local Gods

Greengrass

Joe, the retired blacksmith always wore a dark shiny suit and a hat which was never taken off, even indoors. The smoke blackened hat combined with deep furrowed laugh wrinkles around his eyes were his trademark features. Always the kind word to friend and neighbour as he doffed the hat and winked in salute. He had it figured out that the human race never really solved any problems, but could outlive most of them, given time, which he claimed to have in plenty. Never a man to hurry. He was old now and could remember a time when magpies were scarce. He even had a rhyme for them 'One for sorrow, two for joy, three for a girl, four for a boy', but no one had ever seen more than two at the same time. In any event, he had the countryman's love of nature and an overriding interest in the natural world. He knew everything that could be known about the river. His was a life well lived and he loved angling above all else. He knew every bend in the river, the variations in current, each dark pool and what it was likely to produce in catch. Day or night, he was reluctant to depart from its banks without the reward of at least one speckled brown trout in his kit-bag. He could manufacture casting flies from all sorts of material, ranging from feathers to horse-hair and a selection of these he kept hooked to his hat-band. Now that he had retired and no longer needed to cool his irons, he could truly live by his motto 'A bad day's fishing beats a good day's work.' He loved to relate the true story from decades previously, when a huge pair of Canadian musk-rats (being reared for their pelt) escaped captivity and began to breed along the banks of the river. They grew in numbers and caused untold damage by digging everywhere. In the end, a price was put on their heads and they were hunted and shot to extinction. The last rat was preserved and sent for display to the Natural History Museum in Dublin.

He gave his full attention to the commonplace, especially small birds, from a blue tit in a wall crevice, to a flock of starlings feeding in a frenzy. He could identify which starling acted as the 'look-out' to give warning of danger. At high speed, the birds would rise and scatter in unison to alight on a nearby telegraph wire.

'Ah, that's a murmuration of starlings for ye', giving them their collective term. To vindicate his knowledge he would kindly offer to demonstrate his gift for hypnotizing chickens, controlling bees or getting sheep to sit on their hind legs.

Cycling home past Williamson's sawmills one evening, he was once stopped by a young garda with his notebook poised for a name and address.

'How much time do you have Officer?' enquired the smith politely. This was before reeling off all of his six Christian names, two surnames, occupation in fine detail, finally reaching his long and complicated address.

'How am I doing so far Sergeant?'

The member of the force scratched his head.

'Well ... let's see. So far I've got William, Joseph, John, Wesley. What were the rest again? Ah, never mind. There seems to be no immediate problem anyway – off home with you now and good luck.'

He had an open mind, always willing to discuss any issue in lively and intelligent debate. He gently explained that his own philosophy was never to worry as;

'In my father's house there are many mansions.'

Maggie May

The little lady from Finnoe was always dressed in black as she manoeuvred her high bike up the hill and down the Main Street. A wonderfully cheerful person she lived in one of the last thatched cottages with a cheerful half-door. She would always bid the time of day, making little of any trouble she had herself. She had a wry sense of humour when appropriate. In addition, she had a wide range of old sayings but she tended to get her metaphors mixed up with hilarious results.

'You can take the horse to the water ... but you can't make him lay an egg' or 'That's a horse of a different kettle full of fish entirely' were but two of her favorites.

But she epitomized the old wisdom and was ever ready as a sacred duty to do you a favour if she could. In describing just how ill her sister was, her innocent reply was 'Poorly ... she's in bed with the doctor.'

She had been a mid-wife in her prime and had cures for every ailment known to mankind. These could range from a cure for warts which involved eating boiled nettles, to tying a silk handkerchief with salt around the neck to cure a sore throat. For ailments with no obvious cures such as rheumatism, she would recommend that the sufferer carry the right foot of a hare in their left pocket or put a pair of corks under their pillow. She had a full range of advice for all aspects of living, down to what colour socks to wear for luck and she had credibility as people tended to do what she suggested to no ill effect.

Maggie was a great woman for funerals. She would be the first to the corpse's house to help make tea and serve bottles of stout. She believed in a 'dacent wake' with not too much of a show of grief. And always the last word of comfort: 'Ah poor ould Mick ... it was sudden.' She always said she would like to have her own funeral before she died so that she would know who came to pay their respects, who didn't, and treat them accordingly in the time left to her. She somehow managed to combine the conflicting qualities of shyness and curiosity with the latter becoming more dominant on acquaintance. She never had a begrudging word about anyone. However, if someone

did speak out of turn, she did have a gentle put down;
  'Friend, when you're speaking foolish ... speak easy.'

Munster Fusilier

Bill, the proud old soldier and original contrarian always
sat alone on the same stool at the counter of the Green
Bar endlessly foostering with a well stuffed pipe. He had
survived the horrors of the Somme in World War One.
He had even taken elocution lessons from an Oxford
don in the trenches which gave him an oddly distinctive
way of articulating whatever was on his mind. This was
particularly the case after a few drinks on a Wednesday,
which was pension day for the World War One veterans.
He would take up his position on the high stool ordering
a 'ball of malt' and quoting Samuel Johnson:
  'There is nothing which has yet been contrived by
man, by which so much happiness is produced as by a
good tavern or inn.' Now this was one long sentence for
him and he didn't always get it right first time, but when
in the frame of mind for it, he was capable of starting
an argument with a snowman. As he sat there nursing
his bottle of stout, he'd be damned if he was going to
listen to any old guff from some young upstart at the
bar. He would earwig on conversations, listening out
for anything that didn't conform to his own sensibilities.
He would then feel duty bound to interrupt by clearing
his throat and as soon as he had complete silence and
full attention of the house he would announce;

'Do you know what it is I'm going to tell you ...'

Only to be distracted by two sniggering youths at the back. He would glower at the pair before addressing them;

'With reference to your previous remark, I feel compelled' or 'Given the considerable exuberance of your verbosity!'

Oilcan Ollie

'Ollie' was a gifted mechanic and garage owner. He preferred the simplicity of the combustion engine to the dark complexities of human beings. In a town where people's regard for machines was purely functional, his engineer's brain and mechanical talent marked him as a man apart. His garage and petrol pumps were something of a landmark and his trade came from miles around. The garage was noted not only as a highly efficient and busy auto repair shop, but also a drop-in centre, a clearing house for information and chat or even just to listen to the sound of the rain beating down on the tin roof. Two upturned hubcaps which acted as ashtrays seemed to be permanently full of cigarette butts. The chat inside was in a technical language, sprinkled with in-trade words like head gasket, cam shaft or carburetor. If you didn't know the significance of MPT (Miles Per Tyre) or the merits of the Silver Exide (battery) then it was best to say nothing and just listen. Ollie presided from his bunker down in the pit under a tractor, his hand only emerging to request a file, hacksaw or whatever tool the job demanded. The visitors, particularly those who could not indulge in car talk, were not encouraged to loiter too long. One of his most frequent clients was a local tinker who had purchased a pick-up truck previously. Almost once a week, this man came by to air his concern over a rattle in the 'sauce-pipe' or some noise coming from the 'suspenders'. Ollie was highly amused but a drop of oil from the billy-can usually solved the problem. He had a big generous face with a 'port wine stain,' supposedly acquired from swallowing a glug of petrol whilst siphoning a fuel tank in his youth.

A creature of habit, he took two aspirin each morning, 'just in case' he got a headache from the noise. His special expertise was dismantling cars that had long since passed by their usefulness. He would extract the engine for parts and the body would be passed to anyone who required it as a rain proof hen-house for the end of the garden. Totally absorbed in his trade, Ollie worked long hours alone and would take on just one vehicle at time, which then duly received his undivided attention. Not many people possessed cars, so he had an intimate working knowledge of every vehicle in the parish. He would talk to the cars as he worked on them and locals would sit in just to hear these 'one to one' conversations. It was easy to tell when the job was going well. Ollie would whistle slowly at the beginning of the job. As he made progress, he produced stranger musical noises such as trumpet and bugle impersonations. With the end of the job in sight, he would break into song for a finish, but this was not always the case. Down in the pit trying to loosen a rusty nut in the chassis of a old Ford Prefect. He could be heard to mutter:

'Come out, ya hoor ya!'

Then after a long duration as the spanner was dropped.

'Yerra, how could you be right anyway, with that ould b****x that owns ya.'

The owner of the vehicle was an ageing curate who was totally devoid of a sense of humour. He had dropped in to see how matters were progressing and he was less than impressed with this monologue.

The Speaker

"I'm a rambler, I'm a gambler, I'm a long way from home,
And if you don't like me, well leave me alone.
I'll eat when I'm hungry, I'll drink when I'm dry,
If moonshine don't kill me, I'll live till I die."

This was the song and that was as much as he knew of it. 'Speaker' was a poet, philosopher, raconteur and observer of life, who behaved as if talking to himself but made sure his remarks were heard by all. A man of extremes and contradictions, as complicated as the fifth act of a Shakespearian tragedy. In a conformist culture where individualism was not always appreciated, he stood out like the proverbial 'beacon in a bog.' To us kids, he seemed both daring and immortal. The grown-ups thought that he was daft and were dismissive, but this only added to his aura. He liked to be non-conformist and outrageous, describing himself as 'the man they couldn't hang.' He could be seen seven days a week at his perch on the bridge, whistling a tune or holding wise council. He craved an audience and claimed to be an anarchist, which was meant to either impress or frighten. For a small sum he even would play the tin-whistle and for a further consideration, he might stop.

He was usually garbed in standard dark green FCA overcoat, neatly tied across his tummy with binding twine. His cap leaned to the Kildare side, over a gaunt face that was as seasoned and brown as a sod of turf. In his younger days he was the local odd job man. He was good with animals and had spent much time in the kennels, working with the greyhounds. His previous job as a rat-catcher in the mill gave him a less benign exposure to the animal kingdom. He had been a part-time everything, including gravedigger. Although life had hollowed him out a bit, he still retained a nobility of spirit. Now from the high hill of old age, he had long given up work on the basis that he needed time to think.

'The only two certainties that I know of,' he would muse. 'Is that enough is never enough and time flies. You can wear it on your wrist or spend it, but you'll not control it.'

He dwelled in a moral universe that was truly his own. 'Anybody can just sit here on the bridge all day doing nothing,' he cited. 'But to really get something out of doing nothing, you have to work at it. Like anything, it takes practice.'

He spent long periods pondering such mysteries as – 'Do fish sleep?' Lost travellers looking for directions would receive the less than helpful advice: 'Well if I were going there, I wouldn't start out from here.' He had the full range of prejudices. He was 'agin the Governmint,' whoever was in power. Neither had he time for 'Church, Chapel nor Meeting.' He held strong opinions on everything and when risen, he could curse in flowing Irish and English for a full five minutes, never pausing to use the same word twice. He had long concluded that the best person with whom he could indulge in truly intelligent conversation was himself.

But even as he tried to outwit the clock, the drink would get him in the end. His kingdom was the bridge. He felt more secure there as he liked to keep the town's pubs as a buffer between himself and the graveyard on the Nenagh road. Apparently he didn't intend making that particular journey whilst sober. He thus became a conversion target for some of the evangelical ladies returning from devotions. Oftentimes, he received the unwarranted attentions of a devout lady who was venomous in her personal disdain for the demon drink.

'Speaker, are you still here? I'd swear you'd drink the cross off the back of an ass. 'How can you stomach all that stout and you knowing full well that rats have been seen swimming around in those beer vats above in Guinness' in Dublin.'

'Rats?' says Speaker.

'Rats,' says she.

'Swimming around all day in porter? Be the Holy, Mussus,' says Speaker, peering wistfully into the river. 'You know, sometimes ... I wish ... I was a rat!'

For all his faults, he still personified the classical definition of a philosopher, namely, a lover of wisdom.

These are just five, from the people of a small town with as many home grown dreamers, vagrants, fireside philosophers and street prophets as ever set foot on any stage. It would take a (bigger) book to summarise all the characters around the place. As anywhere, there were boring and downright nasty people as well. There were a few silent types, to whom life had granted few favours and to judge by their demeanour they were not about to bestow any either. There were begrudgers as elsewhere, those who suffered from 'Irish Alzheimer's', in that they had forgotten everything except their grudges. If someone were perceived to be rising too fast above their deemed position, you might hear the odd barbed comment such as, 'Tis, far from stiletto high heels that wan was reared' or 'Sure I can remember when they didn't have a pot to piss in.'

In the words of Samuel Johnson 'The Irish are a fair people ... they never speak well of one another.' But nobody paid much attention. For us kids growing up, it was the droll witty folk who held centre stage in Borris.

SMALL TOWN LIFE

'O my small town of Ireland, the raindrops caress you,
The sun sparkles bright on your field and your Square
As here on your bridge I salute you and bless you,
Your murmuring waters and turf-scented air.'
                                        – John Betjeman

As like a Thomas Hardy novel, it was both urban and rural. If you left your house by the back door you were in the country and if you left by the front you were in the city, almost. To a young child in the confused business of growing up, it seemed a cosmopolitan place at the centre of its own small world. There were community halls, like the David Clarke Memorial hall on Mill Street and Brereton's hall at the Fair Green, catering for a wide range of activities which were complimented from time to time by various travelling shows and circuses. The travelling cinema paid the odd visit, setting up in a marquee in the Square for a week once a year. The serpentine street had three fine churches of cut stone, each catering for the traditional denominations of the townspeople. There were two old hotels, the Hibernian and the Central and a lodging house for vagrants on Tower Hill which charged 1s to sleep on your back and 6d to sleep on your side. The two main banks in Ireland, the Munster & Leinster Bank and the National Bank, both had branch offices on the street. The fine imposing exteriors suggested that they were the preserve of the elite. Few townspeople, beyond the doctor, the solicitor or the big farmer deemed themselves affluent enough to enter these hallowed halls. The main bank had a staff of four. The jovial manager had gone 'native' after a few years there, liked a drink and concluded many of his deals in the nearby hostelry. He was often heard to remark that he felt sorry for all the teetotalers in Borris because as he said, 'When they get up in the morning, that's about as good as they're going to feel all day.' The first bank telephone had been installed a year previously. A helpful notice was mounted on the wall alongside it, giving a set of complicated instructions for usage, down to the final: 'When finished, replace headset. Do not turn handle.' However, neither the old manager nor his assistant manager could answer or make outgoing calls, leaving all aspects of the new technology to the bright young junior in the office. He would surely go on to become a general manager some day. The small post office was a busier hub of mundane commerce and the Postmistress (in deference to her social standing) ran the business with ruthless efficiency, taking lip from nobody. There was always a hushed queue and the minimal small talk was punctuated only by the sharp thud of the clerk's brand on the ink pad. She exuded a crusty kindness but 'woe betide' anyone who tried to skip the queue. Her's was real power. From here, six postmen embarked daily to every corner of the parish on their bikes. Any fit schoolchild could earn sixpence a time by delivering telegrams locally. There were 27 telephones in the parish and subscribers were not expected to make trunk calls after 10pm unless in a dire emergency as this entailed the postmistress leaving her bed to make the connection.

The fire brigade had five hardy part-timers on call but didn't have a fire engine. The fire hose was housed in a long wooden locker along a wall on Main Street, suitably painted bright red. In the event of an emergency – mostly chimney fires – they had a hand cart to bring the hose down the street and attach it to the water mains. Afterwards, they usually spent more time drinking tea in the grateful householders parlour than they spent putting out fires. They were paid by the hour so obviously they had to be extra vigilant in case the fire reignited.

The town had no less than fourteen licensed premises, with more than a hint of competition between the publicans. In his hotel, the regal Gar would enquire politely from his customers as to how the opposition were faring that night. He was not guaranteed a truthful response. He was soft spoken and diplomatic in his style which belied a steely business head. He had a near permanent collection of gloomy commercial travellers, young bank clerks, apprentice vets and bookie's clerks staying at the hotel. On winter evenings, after a feed of hairy bacon and distilled cabbage, they would gather around the Spartan delights of Gar's three-bar electric fire to play cards. He was wily and his trust had to be earned over time. A Limerick horse dealer once called in to enquire about lodgings and was shown to the one vacant room.

'How's this one for you, Sir?' enquired Gar curtly. The room was small and neat but dreary. Each party seemed distrustful of the other. The cattle dealer hesitated.

'God, that window is fierce small. How would I get out through there quickly enough in an emergency?'

'Oh, there'll be no emergencies, Sir. You pay a week in advance!' the host retorted curtly.

At the bridge end, Maude ran her pub and grocery according to her own norms. Closing time in Maude's was more of a lock-in than a go home. She was a proud woman and she kept a close eye on the rival publicans. On Monday mornings, she would carefully count the empty beer kegs left out for collection by the CIE lorry. If it were obvious that she happened to have less than her main rival, then she would add a few spare ones, which the lorry driver knew were display models only.

The publicans were never totally dependent on the bar trade (from a population of 856) and quite often the small bar was an adjunct to a grocery or a butcher shop. In most cases they also had another line such as a bit of land, a few cattle or at the very least a couple of pigs fattening on stale porter out the back. If you were having a drink in Foley's pub, chances are it would be under the salty one-eyed stare from half a pig's head on the counter or to the animated chirps of a dozen day old chicks peeping out through the circular holes of their cardboard prison. In the dark pub interiors, the predominant colour was brown, ranging from the dark brown of cut plug tobacco, to the smoky yellow brown of the ceiling and attendant flypaper. Toilet facilities where they existed were spartan. The lavatory in the back yard was indeed a curiosity best located by the smell of Jeyes Fluid disinfectant. A small wooden structure with a corrugated roof replete with sturdy enamel bucket under a wooden seat. A few weeks copies of the *Nenagh Guardian* helpfully dissected provided the supply of toilet paper on a spike!

In many cases, the stout was bottled in an outhouse at the rear of the pub. The beer casks were made of wood with a bung hole in the side, in which was inserted a wooden chip called a 'Bobbin'. To be capable of 'tapping' a barrel was a skill held in high esteem, as the consequences of a mistake would manifest immediately, in a gush of precious beer towards the ceiling. Although both money and jobs were in short supply, drink was relatively cheap. Arthur Guinness & Co. enjoyed a complete monopoly on drink which was supplied (following cash payment only-no credit) in oak casks by the firkin, each of which contained eight gallons. Three varieties of Guinness were available - single, double and treble - X otherwise' known as the pint of plain. A useful barometer of inflation in rural Ireland was the price of the pint of stout itself. In 1957 it cost 1/6d or about 10 cents. This was a time when the average wage (for those lucky enough to have a job) was £6-10s per week. For those who couldn't afford the pint, the 'medium' (three quarters of a pint) was the cheapest alcoholic drink on the market, 'make mine meejum' was the single most popular order. The ladies' drink was port or sherry, to be sipped discreetly in the dark little snug. Pub hours were 10am to 10pm, seven days a week with an archaic law in relation to Sundays. Under the 'Bona Fide', a consumer had to reside three miles or more from the pub, the idea being that only travellers in need of refreshment could drink. Sunday after Mass was the countryman's drinking time so the 'Bona Fide' law was ofttimes the subject of considerable mileage miscalculation. People drank less than today but spent much more time at it, gossiping over half empty glasses in dimly lit bar rooms pondering such topics as the weather or the price of cattle.

There was a busy creamery, which seemed to have an endless queue of tractors, lorries, asses and carts each with its quota of milk-churns. Jack'o manned the delivery hatch and his special skill was making himself heard above the pure din. We had a fine garda station manned by a sergeant and two gardaí complete with trusty bicycles. The gardaí worked in shifts of four hours morning duty and four hours night duty and by virtue of the fact that they all lived in the town there was little they didn't know. The resident sergeant kept an unerring eye on everything and anything, from poachers to late drinkers, from red diesel to ragwort. There could be no breach of the Noxious Weeds Act 1936 on his watch. He had the gimlet eye of an accountant and nothing escaped his ken. He was no 'Lugs Brannigan' (the legendary Dublin based garda sergeant of Borrisokane origin) but then he didn't need to be too physical. A stolen bicycle would have been the highlight of the week and oddly it seemed to be the same victim each time. The owner, a harmless but attention seeking individual would rush to the barrack in umbrage.

'I looked around me Sergeant, and there it was ... gone!'

In fact it was not the bicycle missing but the pump, which was constantly being stolen and subsequently returned by some young prankster. One of the sergeant's less onerous tasks was to measure rainfall in a specially installed rain gauge in the back garden and take daily note of the level. He loved the paperwork and the meticulous filing of reports. This clerical zeal was not shared by his assistant – Mac – so the sergeant had to keep a close watch on all paperwork. One Fair Day, Mac was called to the Cloughjordan Road where a tinker's horse had been found lying dead. After consulting those present, he couldn't find anyone who could spell Cloughjordan for his report. So to avoid any further embarrassment when the sergeant would inevitably scrutinise the file, he got three tinkers to drag the dead horse around the corner into the Main Street, which he subsequently filed in his report as the scene of the incident. The highlight of both their careers was undoubtedly the surveillance and discovery they made of the biggest cache of poitín ever assembled in the parish. Barrel after barrel of the mountain dew was painstakingly removed to the barrack yard to retain as evidence when making charges. However the gardaí did not count on the determination of the local moonlighters who to their huge embarrassment, repossessed every single barrel in a well tuned clandestine operation during the wee small hours of night. To add to their discomfort, a reporter and cameraman arrived down from Dublin to photograph the forlorn barrack yard for a front page article which appeared in the *Evening Press*.

THIS SPORTING LIFE

The concept of sport was very broad indeed, embracing any code that combined the elements of physical activity and competition. This could range from the local version of rounders, to playing 'ducks and drakes' by skimming small flat stones across a flooded mill pond. Historically there had always been tremendous interest in all sport. A whole variety of sports could claim a traditional foothold to greater or lesser degrees. Apart from field sports like game shooting, fishing and hunting, there was boxing, coarse rugby, football and cross country running. Even cricket had been popular at one time. Fast bowler Malachy Hough from Uskane was a local legend. His style and effectiveness became known to the extent that he was invited to 'Lords' cricket ground in London to play an exhibition match. He turned it down because it was just sport and he had more practical matters to attend to, such as milking the cows.

The farmers kept horses for both work and sport. The Lower Ormond Hunt had the roads to themselves and on one could hear the noisy posse, long before seeing them heading down the Main Street. Horse mad farmers of all shapes and sizes would present themselves, riding animals of every make and description, alongside a pack of baying hounds. The dress code ranged from the sartorially elegant to the downright bizarre. One colourful character was recognizable by a stem of holly in his hat at the annual meet. He was usually well drunk on whiskey and people marvelled at his ability to stay on horseback. Organised sport, particularly sports involving some form of wager or bet were well established. The annual 'point to point' races were held at the racecourse at Kylenagoona near Borris Wood. The wood was once vast, providing ample cover for 'Brennan on the moor', the famous rapparee, to hide from the yeoman back in the 18th century. The course constituted 100 acres of reclaimed land. At its centre, was the last remaining part of the original wood, a fairy fort which couldn't be disturbed. Flags, bunting and a vast array of colour would adorn the course to greet the multitudes travelling from all over Galway, Clare and Offaly. The event was sponsored by the Ormond Hunt but the real mastermind was the landowner, Din. He was a very ordinary citizen, but on race day he was transformed into a virtual knight of the realm. On the morning of the race, Din now transformed into a virtual 'bon viveur' would stylishly emerge through a throng of enquirers outside his house on Mill Street corner. His valuable opinion was sought on all aspects of the event including the favourites, the form, the going and his own best tips. Dressed in a smart check suit, dickey bow-tie and sheepskin coat and replete with a Cuban cigar, he spoke with an air of authority. Whenever he reached into his deep trouser pockets, a pair of red braces became momentarily visible. Just the braces, as it was universally accepted that a man willing to take risks would not wear a belt along with braces just to keep his trousers up. He looked every inch the admiral of the fleet, as he embarked in his dark green 1953 Ford Zephyr - Mark Six to carry out his official duties at the meet. The days events normally didn't go off without with some form of melee on or off the course.

Once a group of tinkers fought to the last man and woman standing, with the fight culminating in the river itself. In some respects it was as well the meet was held just once a year. Greyhound racing, particularly coursing was very popular with huge numbers attending the annual meet at Finnoe. McKenna's kennels in the Square had trained a string of national champions beginning with 'Prince of Bermuda' in 1958. One of the secrets of legendary trainer Ger McKenna's great success was that the dog's drinking water always came from the fountain in the square – that never changed – whether they ran at a coursing just out the road or the White City stadium in London.

There was a much used ball-alley and a fine hurling

field adorned with what was reputed to be the best sod in Munster. Its location was perfect, backing on to the Main Street and the Cloughjordan Road, with a choice of at least four separate entrances from the town. This was the scene of many fiercely passionate hurling matches, drawing large crowds, particularly when Borris were up against neighbouring Lorrha in a championship game. The supporters were the most demanding people in sport. Players and teams came in for strong criticism and if a talented player did emerge, it was always alleged that he had a brother at home who was far better. Failing that, no matter how good he was, he would never be the player his father or uncle or cousin Willie were. A decade earlier, Galway man Anthony James Reddington had cycled across the bridge of Portumna from Connaught to Munster. He went on to become the legendary Tipperary goalkeeper Tony Reddin and it was close to impossible to put a ball past him when he was minding the net for Lorrha. In the week leading up to the match, rumour and speculation would abound concerning the opposition's form, fitness or even vendettas from the previous year. The grass on the pitch would be cut to the butt on the day before with hardly a daisy daring to show its head. The town boys would take up position in Quigley's field to watch out for high flying sliotars. By 3pm the venue would be packed to capacity with tension rising to fever pitch before the throw in. The hair-raising banter which started immediately was directed to the ears of the opposition.

'Come on Knockshee!'

'Squeeze em up, Lorrha!'

Borris had always produced valiant teams who could play tough and tight at the back and fast and furious at the front. They had great players who were both brave and stylish and had distinguished themselves as true sportsmen. Yet tradition and expectation was like a burden for them. Sadly, as a team at senior level they could never seem to find that winning formula. Every year the club produced a calendar featuring a team photo surrounded by little ads from the sponsors. The caption was always the same. It read 'Borrisokane – A Tipperary Gaelic Stronghold.' No one could argue with that. There never seemed to be just one manager in charge but rather a team of about half a dozen mentors who would shout instructions to all and sundry. We knew them as ordinary citizens during weekdays but on the day of the big match they took on a sombre air as befitted the magnitude of the occasion. The most important mentor was the one who could carry the most hurls and balance all of this with a flagon of Cidona under his elbow. From the sidelines came the monotone voice of ever sweating vendor Mickey Connors, loud enough to fill any lull in the general noise levels. He would hold his cardboard box aloft.

'Get your lukie ... lukies ... anyone for the last few Choc Ices now.'

At best, his exhortations fell on deaf ears. At worst, the response would be swift.

'Sit to f**k down Connors, I can't see through you.'

Johnny Kiely was also plying his trade at selling

song-sheets. These were mainly rain and grit encrusted versions of 'The Valley of Knockanure', on a type-form which was all but illegible. If you were really wanted one, they could be picked up for free after the game, once Johnny had the price of a few pints. The Tech girls in their Sunday best would sit out in the front row, sunning themselves and pretending not to notice the attentions of the lads. But too many distractions. The focus would switch to 'Lar Na Pairce' (centre-field) where the action was about to commence. The teams were fully lined up for the parade. The green jerseys versus the blues, striding out purposefully like gladiators in the arena behind the Moycarky Pipe Band. This was championship hurling. Decisive. It was either the road to greater glory or sudden death, for there was no back door. Defeat here meant respite for a full year which was an awful big chunk of any youngster's life. Hopefully the referee would be Philly Ryan of Borrisleigh, the ultimate man in black, who could calm things down with his impish sense of humour. Philly took to wearing glasses for a finish, so the local wits could never suggest that he was in need of a pair.

The ball thrown in and the noise level would reach a crescendo, punctuated by the sharp sounds of ash clashing on ash. With hardly a puck of a ball separating the teams, these contests were played out to their conclusion in this highly charged atmosphere. The play was tough, the pace fast and the going hard but the outcome was usually fair. This was despite the exhortations of some of the more partisan followers on both sides who in an attempt to intimidate the opposition would render warlike cries of:

'Wear off of him, Lack!' or 'Lower the cutting blade, Jim!'

Character was the bedrock of sport and hurling was the game. A tough passionate version of ground hurling it was, with the overhead swing a common feature. This was where passion was poetry in motion, hip to hip. Here was a display of all the skills of stick-work, wrist-work and footwork. There was pulling, bending, lifting and striking. There was jostling, side-stepping and doubling, all played out in cauldron of tribal intensity. The back line functioned like a stone wall, much in the manner of the Tipp full back line of the time, Carey, Maher and Doyle who were known collectively as 'Hell's Kitchen'. They took no prisoners as their motto was 'Thou shalt not pass'. It took speed, skill, determination and a lot more to penetrate this last line of defence but one young player could do this consistently and with style. This was our own local hero 'Mackey' McKenna who had become an established county player. Mackey was low of stature and wide of girth but he hurled with a whirlwind combination of head, hands and heart. His eye to hand coordination was near perfect to the extent the hurley became an extended part of his arm. He was gifted in his timing and would pop up wherever the ball was. The sight of Mackey executing a 21 yard free was awesome, the ball still rising as it bulged the back of the net. His magical solo run up the full left wing of Croke Park, to draw out and open up half the Wexford defence and finally hand pass the ball to Molougney for Tipp's goal was the match winner of the All Ireland Hurling Final and will never be forgotten. He went on to have a distinguished career, garnering every honour in the sport including four senior All Ireland medals but none with Borris. The border location of the parish – just five miles from Offaly (Leinster) and eight miles from Galway (Connaught) made the local community all the more fervent in their deep seated territorial loyalty to Tipperary. It was a case of 'Blue and Gold' forever, and these were indeed glory years for the county team. It was every boy's dream to don the county jersey. In the ten years from 1958, Tipp were to contest in no less than eight All Ireland Hurling finals, winning five. The folk of the Premier County had every right to be proud and happy with their team. Soccer was unheard of then, but what Mick 'Trick' and the regular gallery present at the matches might have made of a sport involving passing backwards to the goalie or players falling down in agony pretending to be injured, is best left to the imagination.

MUSICAL CHAIRS

Nothing captured the soul of the people more than music. The timeless tunes ranged from the melancholy pipers lament to the frenzied energy of a jig or horn pipe. Although not as musical as the Clare people across the Shannon, there were nonetheless a full ensemble of musicians, from singers to set-dancers, from spoon to washboard players, down to chancers who would lilt through a paper covered comb in an attempt to collect coins. There was a demonic accordion player who would play at a frantic pace, his right knee jumping up and down while 'on the button', the accordion doing somersaults in rhythm to the music and all the while a lighted cigarette somehow staying intact in his gob. The kids used to have little side bets on how long the ash would get before it broke off. The jigs, reels and hornpipes had spontaneous titles like 'Nellies Blue Drawers', 'Scatter The Crows' or 'Caileach an Airgead'

(The hag with the money) – a specific reference to a miserly old neighbour living nearby. There were endless lamentable ballads decipherable only by the singer. A request would be put out for a few bars of 'The Night The Old Cow Died'. This was code. Thankfully there was no such song. It was time for the bard to vacate.

The most notable musician the town had produced then was Brendan Hogan, a nationally acclaimed singer who had played all over the world including the Carnegie Hall, New York where he recorded his first LP in 1959. His rendering of 'The Old Bog Road' is still considered to be the finest known recording of the song. It would be heard occasionally on the wireless, during the Walton's programme in between bouts of Din Joe 'dancing' on the radio and we would swell with pride at the mention of our little town on the national broadcaster. People actually did sit and look at the radio in the evenings. The 'wireless' was in a special alcove high up on the kitchen wall and when not playing had small curtains discreetly pulled over it. Contemporary European composer Frank Corcoran was taking his first tentative piano lessons from the diminutive Sr Frances in the local Mercy Convent. The musically gifted Minogue family were playing tributes to their Clare roots, with family members going forth to create and promote beautiful soulful Irish music all over the world. In the McGowan household in Carney, a young Shane sat, both delighted and mesmerized by the musical sounds around him. This was just before the family emigrated to England and Shane McGowan would go on to become a world famous contemporary singer-songwriter. The Puckane man penned the immortal 'Fairytale of New York' and numerous spirited ballads that defined the soul of an exiled generation. Down the road in Coolbawn, Paddy Carroll was busy boiling wood in the making of a guitar for his youngest son, Derry (Darby) who, under the expert guidance of guitar maestro, Joe Cleary, would carve out his own musical niche in the years to come.

There were some hilarious locally composed songs such as 'I dreamt that the porter was tuppence again', which although never quite recording studio material, could be heard from many a crowded bar nearing closing time. We even had a raggle taggle band which appeared miraculously at 12 am on each New Years Eve at the top of Church Road. Led by torchbearers, they would play in the New Year as much to the delight of the local children (watching by the dozen from their bedroom windows) as to the annoyance of the adults who decried the total lack of talent at an ungodly hour. This was a musical entourage which although strong in terms of pitch, was totally lacking the other components of timing, melody and rhythm. But their flair for street theatre overcame all other deficiencies. Uninhibited by the lack of sobriety, they would play out their set with full gusto. One year, Pakie turned up with a set of bagpipes. He was advised by some wag that the local bank manager, was very keen on 'piped music'. On the return journey back up the street, the band made a point of stopping outside the bank house, where Pakie let fly with a robust rendition of 'O'Donnell Abu'. On the lack of any appreciation, they decided to follow up with an encore of 'Slattery's Mounted Foot'. The lights came on upstairs in the bank house and the manager appeared at the front door holding a sleeping child in his arms. He was exhausted after his daily toil at the financial coal-face and was livid at this midnight disturbance. He threatened the gardaí if they didn't put a stop to the din. The ensemble dispersed, with Pakie feeling particularly sore about some lewd remark which the (hitherto respectable) bank manager had made, regarding a suitable bodily location for the permanent placement of the bagpipes.

For the great outdoors, there were plenty of seasonal activities ranging from 'pitch and toss' to 'hunting the hares', with an exodus by foot, bike or car to nearby Lough Derg on the Shannon on hot summer Sundays. A young person's education would have been considered incomplete without knowledge of card games such as 25' and 45' which were played widely. It was vital to know when to play the 'lead' card, as one was expected to remember that the king had been played three tricks earlier. The average family size then was around six children so outdoor pursuits were encouraged. Corporal punishment in school (particularly for the boys) was routine but accepted as normal by parents. It could reach Olympian dimensions in the lead up to big events such as class confirmation but that aspect was considered a mere rite of passage and going home to complain to the mammy and daddy was not an option. Boys and girls were very much segregated at play, in school and church and effectively lived in different worlds.

It was a great place to grow up in, particularly for the

town boys who not being overburdened with work had 'the freedom of the fields, the shelter of the woods' to do their own particular thing. Fights were commonplace but were subject to unwritten codes of honour such as use of the fist but never the boot. If there were enough witnesses around, the 'fight' sometimes amounted to little more than shadow-boxing.

'Mind me coat', the main protagonist would shout. 'I'll have to be dug out of him yet.'

The appropriate response was to put up the fists yelling 'Hold me back lads ... I'll do jail for this'. In time honoured tradition, as soon as enough insults had been exchanged, onlookers would then divide into two groups for the purpose of separating the pugilists. Teenagers had not yet been invented. We had a few 'Teddy-Boys', wide-boys with winkle-picker shoes and Bill Hayley suits, but beyond that, younger people divided themselves into either 'Downtowns' or 'ClockRoads'. The former were from the Main Street and the latter from the Cloughjordan Road. It mattered not that there were a fair few Downtowns teamed up with the ClockRoads and vice versa, it was just for the craic. The catchcry of the day was:

'Eggs and rashers for the Downtown dashers, hay and oats for the Clockroad goats.'

The town kids were idlers and dreamers in the main. The country lads had to work hard on their parent's farms and some would miss school at busy times such as the harvest. One thinks of long summer days in school, looking out the window to the fields, ditches and skies longing for the 3pm bell. The school holidays would come around at an agonisingly slow pace. Six whole weeks of freedom from the tyranny and oppression of National School life! How could a period of time that long be spent. Six weeks away from being stung across the palms by the dreaded 'Bata' (cane). On the last day of school, the hordes would cut loose in a stampede down the hall, out the door to freedom. Down the Nenagh road they went, keeping one eye on the four pinnacles atop the Church of Ireland on the right. It was said that if there were a crow perched on each of the four steeples at the same time, it was a certain omen that someone in the parish had just died. Of course the kids speculated on this theory and enlarged it to include three crows for someone very ill, three magpies for something else and so on. From the intensity of the quickly arranged hurling match or fist-fight in the ball-alley to the harmony of sniggling for eels, trout or brickeens in the river, life had its own easy rhythm.

THE DEAN

'In this little town of ours, there's an energetic man,
who four or five years ago struck upon a plan.
"A cinema," he cried, "a place to entertain."
And so was born the well known Stella Cinema,
Borrisokane.'

Apart from wit, Borris had community spirit going for
it. In the early 50s, the community had come together,
in the main to raise parish funds for St Peter and Paul
church. There were whist drives and a number of
successful carnivals. But Canon Cahill – or to give him
his full title: The Right Reverend Dean Patrick Cahill,
Parish Priest of Borrisokane – had his own ideas. An
intellectual and cultured cleric, when he got an idea into
his head it was very hard to displace, such was his self-
belief. He had brought much to Borris in ecclesiastical
terms. One thinks of his fine baritone voice, the medieval
Gregorian chant he introduced and indeed the many

moving sermons he gave in his time. He was considered direct, a modernist, a leader and as a communicator – ambiguity was not one of his traits. He managed to be conservative in a modern way but he had the wit and intelligence to keep his sermons interesting and topical, normally focusing on the big issues. Occasionally, not often, he touched on the subject of drink and many of the congregation's ears perked up. It was his considered prognosis, that whiskey should only be administered with a doctor's prescription. One of his favourite anecdotes was, 'A drink is nice ... two is enough ... and three ... isn't half enough!'

He was a gritty little man, bald as an egg and full of determination. A lifelong golfer and daily swimmer, he swam in Lough Derg every day of his life, bringing a little pick along with him to break the ice in the cold winter of 1963. This was the year the lake froze over with ice 9" thick from shore to shore. Older residents still recall the thunderous sound of ice finally melting and crashing during the subsequent thaw. But Canon Cahill was a learned liturgist and modern man. He had founded *Molua*, the diocesan journal and for 30 years he edited, managed and published the magazine – now a collector's item. He certainly recognised the social and economic possibilities of a cinema in Borrisokane.

Back in 1936 a man called Vincent Byrne from Birr had rented out the Clarke Hall as a commercial undertaking for £1 a night. He has the distinction of being the first person ever to show films in Borrisokane, even though the venture lasted for just three months.

Films had also been shown in Brereton's Hall in the late 40s but it was a 'hit and miss' operation. One of the hazards was that the seating consisted of rows of long benches (with no backs) and if the heaviest person were to lean back far enough, it could and sometimes did topple the whole row. Although there was not much there for them to eat, hungry fleas were another hazard. Also the floorboards were not the best and were prone to cave in from the pressure of too many patrons on one bench. The Canon, a perfectionist in his own right was keen to have an efficient community backed voluntary operation. Given the conservatism of the era, when both state and church were struggling to control what people thought and saw – and in most instances the clergy were denouncing the evils of cinema and modernity from the pulpit – it was all the more remarkable that in Borrisokane, the parish priest was the mastermind and driving force behind the whole concept. On reflection, it was extraordinary.

At a meeting he outlined his plans to the local committee. The youngest members of the group, Denis Gardiner – and Tony Murphy were most enthusiastic and the idea received overall approval. Next item on the agenda was to choose an appropriate name for the proposed cinema. A number of suggestions were made. The usual names came up – Grand, Royal, Regent, and Regal – but at the behest of Canon Cahill the agreed name would be 'Stella' the Latin word for star. For a clergyman to embrace the dangerous influence of popular cinema in 1956 was unusual if not unique.

'That such an undertaking
be a wonderful success,
A committee must be formed,
and zeal it must possess.
Yes, that is what happened in this town,
a few miles from the Shannon.
Some volunteers came on to help
our parish priest, the Canon.'

- Gerry Slevin

Movie Mania

Into this world in 1957 came the cinema, the greatest living art form of the 20th Century. For a generation of people, young and old, life would never be the same again. The outside world had arrived in black and white and glorious Technicolor. For a town of dreamers, the illusions turned to a flickering version of reality. We sat spellbound in our own dark cave of magic. We thrilled to the chariot race in **Ben-Hur**. We exploded into laughter at the antics of **The Three Stooges**. We grew on the tension of **The Gunfight at the O.K. Corral** and many a cowboy shoot-out. The earliest memories are undoubtedly of those great favourites with the kids – **Laurel and Hardy**, followed a close second by **The Three Stooges** and **Old Mother Riley**. For us young children from a tightly disciplined, close knit community these characters were incredible. Here were fully-grown adults making total idiots of themselves. Poor Stan Laurel never seemed to learn from his disasters and continued to ignore our shouted warnings at each Sunday matinee. This was living proof of what we suspected all along –

that adults were not as smart as they made themselves out to be, nor were we kids so thick either! Certainly the world was a much more exciting place than any of them had ever let on with all their cosy certainties. The enclosed order of childhood was set to change radically as film became so much a part of growing up. In the 1950s black and white world of church and state, the colour and magic of cinema was at work with a staple diet of motion pictures subverting the ground rules weekly.

The early films, particularly the Westerns, were novel at the time and given the local love of melodrama, commanded total audience credibility. Whole new vistas opened up – big skies, canyons, valleys, ranches, thundering stampedes and ghost towns as a backdrop to the pulsating sound of horse hooves and Indian whoops. Monument Valley has never looked so awesome as when viewed over clenched white knuckles from the front row of the Stella. Cowboy culture had its own language, peppered with new words like 'Hombre', 'Gringo', 'Injun', and 'Critter'.

Picture the cliched scene. The lone cowboy rides in desperation and a cloud of dust back to the fort, followed in hot pursuit by a band of whooping blood thirsty Indians. As the unfortunate cowboy finally reaches the fort, the defenders close across the large entrance gates. In the picture house, the back row goes wild.

'Jay's ye can't do that lads … he's one of your own.'

'Bloody awful, they did the very same last night, you know,' says another voice from the middle row.

We kids literally lived from Wednesday to Sunday night and from Sunday night on to Wednesday. The cinema became a culture complete in itself, beginning with the unruly queue for the 'nine-penny rush' at 7.30pm when the front doors opened. We were soon transported far beyond the borders of our small grey town, to faraway lands and different eras of history. The Stella had its own sights, its own distinct sounds and smells and eventually its own rituals. Running through the entrance gates, up the two stone steps and into the foyer. You reach up to Mr Gardiner and Mr Kelly in the box office with your shilling and receive the precious ticket in exchange. Tim and John Egan greet you, as they check your tickets to part the heavy velvet curtains letting you in. You troop down to your own particular seat in the front row – the wooden 'bucket' seats that jump up on their own if no-one is sitting in them 'The Woodners'. The Stella had its own unique smell, a mixture of French polish and pine wax mingled with stale smoke. Its own sounds, even before the show with the wistful strains of Rick Nelson playing 'Poor Little Fool' or Guy Mitchell playing 'She Wears Red Feathers and a Hooley Hooley Skirt' or our own favorite Perry Como singing 'Catch a falling star'. In any event, we kids were safely cocooned from the tiresome constraints of reality. But all of this was just a foretaste of the sheer magic of the lights going down and the curtains parting. Let the show begin!

THE HALL

'Bless this house, oh Lord we pray
keep it safe by night and day'
                          – Helen Taylor

The cinema would be located in the Clarke Memorial
Hall on Mill Street, a short street on the road to Birr.
Mill Street was a busy little place in its own way back
then. You could buy your bag of flour from Tim Heenan
in the corner shop which adjoined the corn mill. You
could have your suit or skirt adjusted by Chrissie Darcy
across the road and then sent to the Connaught Laundry
via Whelans next door. You could have your hair cut
by Toddy Horrigan and get a lifetimes advice unasked
for. Toddy's little cottage was a 'rambling house', a great
place for a card school or local gossip. He would expertly
render the full short back and sides treatment by putting

a bowl over your head to get the shape right, leaving a little wisp at the front. While waiting, you could leave your bicycle across the road for repair to Slevin's Cycle Works, who were well capable of putting patches on top of the existing patches if necessary. Depending on the misdemeanours of the previous week, you could have your confessions heard further up in the old church. Now to top it all a Picture House would soon be opening in the Clarke Memorial Hall.

This building was constructed as a community hall in 1930. It was originally endowed by the last will of the landlord Harriette Clarke of Macclesfield, Chester in 1904. Its purpose was for 'the instruction, education and amusement of the people of the town of Borrisokane, as the Trustees deem fit and proper.' The bequest was quite specific in relation to all aspects, including a stipulation that the caretaker (who must reside within a half mile of the hall) received wages which were not to exceed ten shillings per week. The first caretaker was a diligent man called Willie Gilton. During the tenure of the Stella cinema, the man in charge was Jimmy Meaney of Church Road. The hall itself retains some striking architectural features. Inside, the tapered ceiling was supported by semi-circular iron girders with massive bolts that could conceivably have supported the hulk of the Titanic. Dark green was the predominant colour of the paint-work. Externally there was a worked ashlar cut stone entrance under a hammered keystone and seven dormer windows down each side of the roof. The stone had come from the Bridewell which formerly stood on

Jail Road beside the Fair Green. The hall was already complete with a fire proof projection room at the top of the stone staircase just inside the main entrance, so clearly it had been purpose built as a theatre for film.

According to the *Nenagh Guardian*'s Borrisokane notes dated 3 April 1957:

Borrisokane will have a new cinema on Easter Sunday night when Reverend Canon Cahill P.P. opens the Stella in the Clarke Memorial Hall. The aim of this enterprise is to raise funds for the parish with a view to improving the existing parish church or the building of a new one. Canon Cahill, at a meeting in the Legion of Mary Hall last Sunday appointed a committee to steer the project to success.

Included in this were:
Box Office: S. Gardiner & J. Kelly.
Operators: E. Slevin, P. Heenan & T. Heenan.
Booking films: D.Gardiner.
Collecting & dispatching films: T. Heenan.
Hon. Sec & Hon. Treasurer: PJ Heenan.

For the purpose a new balcony has been erected and 234 cinema seats fitted, an Arc 16 mm projector purchased. A cinema -scope screen has been obtained, the hall decorated and new toilet accessories fitted.

THE JOURNEY

On Ash Wednesday 1957, three members of the committee made a memorable 100 mile trip to Dublin in Son Slevin's lorry with an extensive shopping list for the new cinema. They had a number of calls to make, which included Louis Elliman, film impresario and managing director of Odeon (Ireland) Ltd, to bargain for and purchase the all important cinema seating. Louis Elliman along with Emmet Dalton had only recently concluded the purchase of Ardmore House and 35 acres in Bray for £5000 to finally establish a native film studio. The seating on offer was second-hand but in remarkably good condition. It came from Dublin's legendary Theatre Royal on Hawkins Street that was sadly about to be demolished to make way for an office block. The Theatre Royal was legendary and central to

Dublin's nightlife. It had seating for 3,600 patrons in its beautiful Moorish style auditorium and it was here that the European premiere of the film **High Noon** took place in 1953.

The following was the purchase order:

156 New Pullman seats at Three pounds, ten shillings each.

48 Second-hand (Met) at Two pounds, ten shillings each.

30 Wooden bucket seats at One pound, ten shillings each.

Whilst the three had to share the two cramped seats in the front of the old Dodge truck on their journey to Dublin, they cheerily noted that on the return journey their choice of seats was almost unlimited. Also purchased on this trip was a Horizon 16mm arc projector costing £850 and two large Dousonic speakers for backstage. The final call of the day was to Denis Guiney of Clearys on O'Connell Street for rust coloured velvet curtains. Contact was made with film distributors such as Ward & Anderson, Rank, Sight & Sound, Ron Harris, MGM, United Artists, and 20th Century Fox.

Contracts were drawn up to the effect that for a payment of £80 per annum, the films would be delivered twice weekly in special metal containers (cans) to Bride Foley's on Lower Main Street. Paddy McKenna's Ironworks were given the task of constructing a huge metal frame onto which was stretched a 'state of the art' white perforated screen, only the second of its kind ever used in Ireland. This screen was lovingly covered at the end of each show to prevent any possible damage from other activities in the hall (on non-film nights) such as billiards and snooker. Denis Gardiner, the school teacher was put in charge of selecting and booking the films and at no stage did the Canon exercise any form of censorship. It was good news when Denis recommended a particular film to the class, as there was no way parents would then refuse either the permission or the money to attend. Denis' father Jim was the principle in the boy's school and he would man the box office. For young pupils it was better to have your homework done for the next day because Jim would undoubtably remember if you had bought tickets. Egan's Joinery designed and built the seating platform and balconies. When the seating arrived from Dublin, over 1,300 screws were used in the final assembly. This would have included placing a metal ashtray between each two seats. Two EXIT signs were expertly made by the local handyman using a fretsaw combined with red crepe paper and two red bulbs. These were turned on whenever anyone remembered to do so. An account was opened with the local Munster & Leinster Bank for handling the funds. A printing block (costing 1-16s-6d) was moulded to place the advertised showing in the *Guardian* and the *Midland Tribune* weekly. During the winter months the caretaker became a busy man, stoking up the boiler an hour before each show and ensuring there was sufficient fuel to last. The grassy area around the hall was resown and well trimmed lawns were lovingly maintained throughout the tenure of the cinema.

Edward Slevin Electrical supplied the (Elpico) record player and records for the pre-film entertainment. The records included the National Anthem on 45" which was played nightly after the film. The box office was constructed to the left of the entrance so as to accommodate three ticket collectors comfortably. A mahogany wooden frame was placed on the wall to the right of the entrance, to house the colourful cinema posters. The glass in the bay windows was painted black, both inside and out so that not a chink of external light would intrude during screening. Overhead infrared heating was also installed for the additional comfort of the patrons. That first week of April 1957 was one of frenetic activity with over 30 people working flat out in the Clarke Memorial Hall in order to be ready for opening night the following week.

THE TEAM

For the successful running of the cinema, duties had to be rotated as follows: three projectionists, four ushers and two in the ticket box. The original three projectionists were Ned Slevin, Tim Heenan and Paddy Heenan and they were destined to play a key role in the operation. The 'magic lantern' was the nerve centre, the very foundation of cinema. Here is where light entered a totally dark space through a tiny opening and projected the images from the reel of film onto the big screen at a rate of 24 frames per second. The 'reel' thing was just fast enough to trick the eye, and the brain! Given the level of expertise required, their role was not rotated during the lifetime of the cinema, so two of the trio always had to be present. In effect it was to mean working four nights a week, as up to six film reels had to be painstakingly rewound before each showing. The projectionists had to ensure that the photo-electric cells were aligned and framed. The splicer, arcs and lens had to be checked and their presence was required full-time, given that a snap in the film reel could result in an immediate breakdown. A powerful beam of light was generated by the fusion of two 9" carbon rods which had to be replaced from time to time when the carbons burned out. They worked long hours in the projection room in difficult conditions, particularly with the fumes that emanated from the projector. This became a health issue and some time afterwards, a special flue and chimney was built thereby solving the problem. The original projector held one very large metal spool itself the size of a bicycle wheel. In time this would be replaced by two 35mm projectors for which two new openings (bringing the total to four) had to be cut in the wall.

Just off the main projection room was a little room where the ritual of taking the reels from the cans and preparing them for the projector took place. In the early days, halfway through each film, there would be a sudden bang and splutter as the hall was plunged into inky darkness. This was the first projector running out before the second projector was brought into action. Due to an oversight once, on the changeover, the second half was shown upside down on the screen until the projectionist's attention was captured by the thunderous sound of dozens of feet stamping on the wooden floor. However, over time this team came to perfect the art of timing the switch to the second projector almost seamlessly and without interruption during the show, to the extent that the audience would be blissfully unaware of the changeover. A perfect montage.

Ned Molloy would take charge inside the hall once

the film began having, had prior experience of this in Brereton's Hall. One thinks of the classic role of a cinema floor manager during the showing of a film. At the turn of the century, when James Joyce was manager of the Volta Cinema in Mary Street, a long brush handle was used to reach across and prod any of the rowdy patrons who looked like getting out of hand. Ned didn't need a bargepole strategy. He was extremely popular and used shuttle diplomacy as he weaved his way around the hall with his trusty flash-lamp. On those occasions when the projector broke down, the foot stamping brigade would commence their noisy business and loud wolf whistles would rent the air. Ned would launch his customary appeal for calm until the show resumed. He led by example by keeping calm himself. He would then melt into the background, only to be recalled by the kids in the front row after a shoot-out.

'Come back Ned ... and take away the bodies!'

GRAND OPENING

'Bless these walls so firm and stout,
Keeping want and trouble out.
Bless the roof and chimney tall
Let thy peace be over all'
— Helen Taylor

The Stella Cinema, Borrisokane opened its doors to
an eager public on Sunday April 7th, 1957. This was
a major event, bigger than any fair, hurling match
or election. Bigger even than the dancing bear from
Fossett's Circus, whose amazing antics had the people
enthralled for so long. People travelled from all over
the parish and beyond by bicycle, car, lorry, horse &
trap and shank's mare. Bicycles were stacked six deep
along the green railings outside. The hall's 234 seats
were occupied from early that evening with latecomers

standing in the aisle craning over shoulders to see the action. The team of three projectionists was introduced and took a gracious bow to spontaneous applause before mounting the stone steps to the projection room at the back of the hall. The Dean had prepared a little speech to mark the occasion. He spoke of the history and benefits of cinema, now just 60 years old, the same age as himself. He even mentioned someone called the Lumière brothers in France, whom he said had started the whole enterprise at the turn of the 20th century.

'No one person invented cinema,' he cited, 'but a real community combination of business people and artists.'

The Dean was a man of small stature and as he spoke he seemed dwarfed by the huge curtains draping the screen behind him. The audience was getting bored as most of them were used to hearing him Sunday after Sunday and the wily Dean could sense an element of impatience setting in. As with his sermons, he used one of his witty one-liners to conclude, advising the patrons:

'Not to clap too hard ... it's a very old building.'

As the lights went down, the curtains parted slowly to tumultuous applause and history was in the making.

The feature film was the musical ***Marching Along*** featuring Clifton Webb, Debra Paget and a youthful Robert Wagner. It was based on the life of John Philip Sousa, the world famous American bandmaster and inventor of a musical instrument called the Sousaphone. Born in Washington of Italian origin, he toured everywhere with his 'Sousa Band'. He became known throughout the world as the March King. He had composed more than 100 marches, the best known being 'Liberty Belle', 'Hands across the Sea', and 'Stars and Stripes Forever' ('Hooray for the red, white and blue'). The latter was in fact the US title of this 1952 film. His influence changed the military march style of US armies into the early years of the 20th century. The trailer had featured Norman Wisdom in *Man of the Moment*. The British comedian was to prove a huge hit with local cinema-goers in the years to follow.

The entrance pricing set on that first night was:

Balcony	2/-
Parterre	1/6
The Pit	1/ -
Matinee	9d

It is a fact that in the ten years of the Stella's existence these prices never went up, which tells us something about inflation in this era. Depending on whether you used coal or turf, it was cheaper to go to the pictures than to light the fire for an evening. And it was certainly much more fun than staying at home keeping the cat out of the ashes. The evenings entertainment began with a short, usually *Laurel & Hardy* or the *Three Stooges*. This was followed by the news feature, usually the Pathe News whose logo of the crowing cock was to become most familiar to regular audiences. These newsreels usually consisted of stale news, often up to five years old and likely of more interest the English audience it was filmed for. No one would get over excited by the spectacle of members of the Royal family breaking champagne bottles off the side of ships, smiling film stars visiting hospitals or the dubious delights of the Jersey Flower Show. Mind you, it was the first time local kids had ever seen the 'beautiful game' of football that they called soccer. Stars like Danny Blanchflower playing for teams like Manchester United, dribbling' the ball along the ground but still half expected to pick up the ball and go on a solo run or kick for a long range point, which would have been most difficult in the absence of upright goal-posts. Oddly, the players wore round necks on their jerseys, which was never seen on a Gaelic pitch. Some of them we were told were Irish although we had never heard their names in Michael O'Hehir's breathless reports from Croke Park. However for children (and some adults) who had never travelled outside of a ten mile radius of the parish, some of the items shown could well have been from another planet. In some respects there were historic echoes of a Gaelic order encountering a dominant Anglo world view for the first time.

Films were shown on Sunday and Wednesday nights but such became the demand that Friday nights were added one year later. So essentially it was entertainment three nights per week with the exception of Lent and the Mission. It is recorded that the cinema was closed to mark the death of Pope Pius 12th on October 11th

1958. For many people going to the cinema became as much a part of the routine of their ordered lives as going to church. The cinema had become a huge success both socially and commercially. In its first year it catered for an almost capacity crowd nightly and on St Stephen's night in 1957 there were over 40 patrons standing in the porch in addition. Although the 'House Full' sign went up from time to time it is not believed that anyone was ever turned away after a little negotiation. Next door to the hall, Guilfoyle's stocked up their little sweet shop which did a brisk trade with the cinema-goers, their raspberry ice-creams being a great favourite with the local children. Further up on the Main Street, queues would form outside Teddy Byrne's shop for fish and chips before and after the shows.

It is difficult now to describe the feverish excitement and constant discovery that going to the pictures meant to a generation of schoolchildren. One forever remembers the mixture of ecstasy and terror felt as a steam train came straight at you from the screen, only to dissolve into the next scene leaving you unscathed. Even the 'shorts' seemed colourful and exciting.

A huge cheer would greet the now familiar voice of Edgar Lustgarten announcing **Fabian – Of Scotland Yard**. To emerge on a Sunday afternoon from a matinee with the day still young and find the sun was shining outside was a surreal experience in itself. The cinema didn't just entertain. It took reality and turned it upside down before our eyes and in many respects became a quasi religious collective experience. The impact on a child, of a whole community of people sitting together in the dark focusing their emotions on the main event, a moving film, was enormous. A whole generation of kids, weaned on British comics (such as the Victor, Hotspur, Beano and Dandy) encountered the powerful culture of American films for the first time. It illuminated, educated and motivated young lives and film was recreated daily on the streets and in the fields. And with this exposure to a broad universe, what did the kids think about afterwards? They thought more deeply about their own little town with its nooks and enchanted places, now given characteristics which existed only in the realm of imagination. They say that life imitates art, thus the fort became Sherwood Forest, Chadwick's Wood became the steamy jungle and the river at its shallowest point became the Rio Grande. There were more childish imaginative sub plots invested in the little streets and lane-ways than a lifetimes international experience was ever likely to yield. The kids were the stars, walking around in films directed by their own vivid imaginations. In a staid period in history, young imaginations were set free by the cinema experience. In many respects the cinema had more influence on children than the state and the church put together. It became inevitable that the world would not stay closed for ever and this was the early precursor of the vast changes that would undoubtedly follow. From there on we kids looked to the cinema to broaden our horizons.

THAT FIRST OUTING

For an infant, that first trip to the cinema in the bosom of one's family was an unforgettable life enhancing voyage. It would be seared in the mind forever in the laser light of first experience. The word cinema was not used. For months one heard older siblings excited talk about the 'pictures', pronounced 'pitchers'. We had seen images of these film stars collected from chewing gum wrappers and packets of tea. But one had to ask, 'How exactly does it work ... these moving pictures?' If you have been familiar with pictures in their frames as part of life's learning experience up to now, the idea of moving pictures seemed bizarre. Logically speaking if they moved, why did they not move off the wall altogether and escape. Without experiencing 'the pictures' this was all a mystery.

Sunday matinee time would come around at last with Mother explaining as best she could to her eager young kids as events unfold. Warm greetings at the door.

'First time ... well, well you're in for a treat. Take your seats, folks.'

The sense of adventure and anticipation was palpable. The deep trance of everyday life had found a focus in the interchanging of light and shadow. Everybody sitting in their snug seats, whispering and rustling bags of sweets. You can just make out friends and neighbours in the half light and a red sign with the letters EXIT over the door on the right. The scene is dominated by a huge white screen. If you look directly behind you there is whispered activity high up in the wall at the back. Perhaps that is where God resides so that He can see everything. In an instant total darkness descends. It must be God all right. Grab Mammy's arm and thankfully she's still there. She smiles and pats your little hand. Then from Heaven at the back, a celestial beam of light cuts a path through the surrounding darkness and you hear a low whirring noise. The light is so bright you can't look directly at it but if you follow it on up to the big white screen it's a kaleidoscope of colours. At various points, plumes of blue smoke ascend to linger over the audience below. On screen, a static sheet of official looking paper appears with a squiggle in the middle, only to unveil a majestic roaring lion over the letters MGM and ... we're away. Music, big writing and all the kids in the audience now cheer as the familiar features of two men (one fat, one skinny) in suits too tight for them, waddle down a city street. Always arguing:

Laurel: 'You drank it all – we were supposed to share it!'

Hardy: 'I couldn't help it. My half was on the bottom' or Laurel: 'You never met my wife did you?'

Hardy: 'Yes, I never did.'

Slapstick fools but such fun. You are carried along in a trance by the action up front. Life is unfolding, only louder, bigger and more exciting than your everyday experiences. For the rest of the show, reality, memories and dreams merge together in a colourful mix of agony and ecstasy. And you first experienced the fundamental delight of cinema, that is the thrill of being scared out of your wits while knowing yourself to be totally safe and sound.

Local Cinema Culture

In social terms, the cinema became an integral and influential part of life in Borrisokane. The grey old town had got its first sprinkle of stardust and film was to touch and move the people in ways they never thought possible. It triggered memories. It aroused feelings. None could be indifferent to this exciting new medium. The back page of the *Nenagh Guardian* would be eagerly perused to find out what was showing at the Stella in the coming week. Although the theme running through each film was ultimately the battle between good and evil, reading the *Guardian*, this could be further divided into a few sub-themes. Either the journey, a stranger comes to town or perhaps somebody's life story. The most junior reporter was given the job of coming up with the home spun by-lines:

> Suspense, thrills and excitement as the Scotland Yard detective tries to track down the sadistic killer in the fog, but is the hunter about to become the hunted?

Josie the orphan girl is caught between her love for her pet sheepdog and fear of her domineering old uncle. As she takes to the hills in the dead of winter, a storm approaches.

A man dies in a plague ridden village in Mexico and in his efforts to investigate, Rick Regarde stumbles across a mad Nazi scientist's wicked conspiracy.

Adjectives like cracking, rip-roaring and swash-buckling were sprinkled about liberally.

But in addition to artistic acclaim, the cinema was also highly successful in commercial terms. In the five years from 1957 to 1962, the Stella made a profit of £4,026-16, thereby exceeding its objective to raise parish funds. Sunday night was the busiest and best night for business. Many of the all time classics were shown including **Casablanca**, **The Thirty Nine Steps**, **All Quiet on the Western Front**, **A Town like Alice**, **The Spiral Staircase,** and **The Third Man** to mention but a few. These were in addition to a staple diet of what we now call B-movies with such evocative names as **Red Planet Mars**, **The Attack of the Fifty Foot Woman**, **How to make a Monster**, **The Brain Eaters** or **Taza – Son of Cochise**. The face of one Ronald Regan would have been most familiar in various Western roles (many of which would have benefited from a little more time in the cutting room). It was well known that Dublin Zoo (who bred the finest lions in captivity) had supplied the famous MGM lion shown at the start of each of their films. A lot of these films were abject nonsense, pure 'pot-boilers' that quickly ran out of steam, but this didn't matter a great deal to the faithful patrons. In the whole experience of habitual cinema-going the sense of partaking and belonging was more important. A good film was a bonus not necessarily an expectation. Its critical acclaim was not very important, as long as it provided a bit of distraction. What was important was the ritual, the arrangements, the journey, the bag of sweets, the packet of cigarettes, who you accompanied there, who you might meet, who was present and who was absent. Given that the patrons didn't take the whole business too seriously, the sense of humour and fun that prevailed never deserted them. In case the short films did not materialise with the main film reel, a few reels of *The Three Stooges* were always kept in reserve, giving rise to a full month of *Three Stooges* shorts at one stage. As one old character remarked on leaving the hall:

'The Three Stooges ... Man Dear ... if I see one more episode of those Three f***ing Stooges, – I'll write the script meself! Do they live in Borris full time? How much is it costing ye to keep them above in the Griffin Arms?'

Over time in the Stella the audience became the 'stars'. On a Sunday night in the harsh winter of 1962, Jimmy had trouble trying to ignite the boiler and the temperature inside the hall began to drop rapidly after dark. The stock of coal had been depleted and there would have been none but for the heroic efforts of his neighbour Noel Cooley. Noel's extended family ran 'Cooley's Coal' from the Northside of Dublin and they saved the day at a time of scarcity. The feature film was *It's a Wonderful Life* featuring James Stewart as a man who somehow gets a second chance. In a key moment in the film as Stewart is going through his own crises, a heavy snowfall begins. The boiler in the cellar would not ignite so the cold was really beginning to bite with the audience too but the onset of snow in the film brought matters to a head. Danny Shan dashed from his seat, suddenly remembering the 'in-lamb' ewes left in the field. A delegation went in search of Jimmy, to see if the boiler could be started, even at this late stage. Luckily Mrs McGarry, who lived next door, brought in a few blankets which were passed around as the remaining audience huddled in their seats for warmth. But the film was considered so beautiful that most were content to remain on, right to the bitter cold, but happy ending. There was a happy ending as the hero instead of ending his life found redemption in the bosom of his family.

Many young people learned proper smoking techniques at the cinema. There were certain norms to be adapted. For example, only a passive thinking actor would smoke a pipe and a rich actor would smoke a big cigar. Humphrey Bogart was the doyen of screen cigarette smokers down to the way he held a cigarette, fingers on top, thumb underneath. His whole body language made smoking a natural extension of his machismo and the teenagers in the hall watched every billow for style.

Regulars by now had their own 'special' seats and it became important to know the social strata inside the cinema hall. To sit in a designated seat was considered extremely rude and sometimes gave rise to a short argument just before the show. Ned the manager would invoke his own brand of democracy by ensuring that the regular occupant was duly seated whilst quietly explaining the mechanics of the system to the stranger.

One very keen film-goer, 'The Boss' McKenna had his special seat where he had ample room to park his crutches and stretch his legs. The Boss rarely missed a film and he always expressed his satisfaction on leaving the hall. Further in on the same row was Jack Meagher who sat through the cowboy films contentedly puffing his pipe giving the odd comment when matters were going to his satisfaction. He professed that he liked going out to the pictures to get 'the smell of the house' off himself. As far as he was concerned, it was a great cure for cabin fever. Oddly he never empathized with the leading character. He preferred to study the supporting cast. The 'Gear' made a beeline for the pictures on his scooter every Friday night, often reaching speeds of up to 17 mph so as not to miss the trailer. He had a specially designed metal box built in to the bike which housed his penknife, pipe and plug tobacco. He cut a rare figure astride the old scooter with his elegant trench coat, peaked cap and pipe rigid in his gob. His speech itself was pure mechanical parlance. Man and machine intermingled. He spoke of himself as 'the old machine' with 'a right few miles up on the clock'. You could locate his beloved scooter parked at the cinema railings by his faithful sheepdog sitting on sentry duty. The seats immediately alongside Molly the doctor's housekeeper were always empty. Unfortunately she had a chronic hearing problem. She was as deaf as a bodhran and would inevitably become confused during a film, leading her to persistently tap on the shoulder nearest to her at regular intervals to enquire as to what was happening on screen. The whistler from Carney would always turn up for the cowboy films to demonstrate his skills. He spent his day in charge of a large flock of sheep on Carney Common with the help of two sheepdogs. During the film, with his two little fingers placed in the corners of his mouth he would emit a high pitched whistle as soon as the first 'steer' appeared through a cloud of dust on the screen. He was completely in his element for **Lassie Come Home** (which featured an 11 year old Elizabeth Taylor) and **Son of Lassie**. Sean Egan and his pals found their own way into the cinema. They climbed the boiler house flat roof and entered through a side window. They sat quietly most nights watching the movie in reverse on the far side of the screen. Dean Cahill usually slid in quietly when the film was in progress. His influence was mild like the moon, always in the background, keeping a paternal eye from a chair in the centre aisle, until he fell asleep in the chair.

Once the audience settled down, they generally sat there in deep space with all the dreamy focus of the denizens of a Chinese opium den, until the last quarter of the film when they began to twitch and shuffle. Over the years they would become well-educated film buffs. Given their traditional love of a good play, an intelligent well paced film such as **His Girl Friday** (to all effects and purposes a play on screen) was always well received. If you were standing in the middle aisle, it was not uncommon to have two completely different reactions coming from each side. They were a very discerning audience although critical faculties could be suspended in the interests of happiness. They generally offered their views which could be good, bad but never indifferent to the management on leaving the hall. Given the novelty of the experience, the reviews were mostly positive. Word would circulate in Toddy Horrigan's, the barber, that there was a 'right' film on the other night.

'Yer man John Wayne bet the solid lard out of this Indian'. Or alternatively, 'it was a total disaster – nobody got killed!' Wag Quigley was a less demanding connoisseur. The Wag's definition of a good film was one that he could fall asleep during and not have missed anything when he woke up a half-hour later, i.e. a slow moving film.

But as time went on, it became important to be able to 'talk' a film properly to describe exactly what happened in glowing detail. It would of course be a mistake for any would-be film critic to try and upstage their audience by quoting details of a film seen at the nearest rival the Rialto cinema in Nenagh, just ten miles away. The Rialto was all very well in its own right. It was a fine, purpose built 900 seat cinema operating since 1947. It had its own shop, majestic marble floors and a winding stairs leading to a palatial balcony. It had smart usherettes dressed in green uniforms replete with little pillbox hats. By Borris standards, it was positively plush and cosmopolitan but somehow lacked the homely intimate feel of the Stella. No, it would be a mistake to start spoofing about the Rialto, with its latest colour films and the familiar seashell opening slowly to introduce a yawn inducing litany of corny and local ads suggesting we have a drink in O'Meara's Hotel after the show. Bah!

THE DEAN'S DINNER

'We now must say goodbye and wish you all success,
You're certainly doing a wonderful job to bring us
happiness,
And as the year is ending, in wind and hail and rain,
We couldn't be more comfy than in the Stella,
Borrisokane'
                                                    –Gerry Slevin

As acknowledgement of their efforts throughout the year, the Stella committee was invited to dinner in the Griffin Arms hosted by Dean Cahill during Christmas week. This was a lavish affair and one of the social highlights of the year. The proprietor, Mr Griffin himself, formerly Lord Huntingdon's footman would don his red evening jacket which normally appeared only on royal occasions. A seven course meal would be served, to include such delicacies as hare soup. It was a grand soiree and a 'sing-song' would continue into the late hours. It was traditional for someone to give a rendition of 'The Hunt', a song which featured the exploits of many of the characters in the locality. To mark the success of the cinema, a beautiful poem was penned by a local young journalist, Gerry Slevin, who would go on to become editor of the *Nenagh Guardian*. The poem was subsequently put on tape to background music –

The Humming Chorus – for annual performance at the 'end of year' party.

Although most of the committee were teetotallers, one of the members had a good deal more whiskey than was intended, more by accident than by design. His state of inebriation did not become apparent, until he offered to go to the upstairs bedroom to collect the coats. When he had not returned after some 20 minutes, a search party was dispatched to find him asleep between the two single beds on which the coats were left. Two volunteers immediately offered to escort him home but when they turned right outside the front door, (knowing that their charge lived down the street to the left) it was soon realized that the escorts were in worse shape themselves, for they were truly 'trí na ceile' (i.e. very drunk). Our poor friend was escorted down to his house but another problem now arose – he had no front door key. He lived with his puritanical sisters who took a very dim view of the demon drink at the best of times. This problem seemed to have been solved with the sudden appearance of a neighbour, well known for his nocturnal appearances on the street. This man rendered his assistance and in a feat of some skill and dexterity managed to prise open the downstairs window. The inebriate was hustled in through the open window but unfortunately just inside was a table adorned with ornaments, vases and framed photographs. The whole 'shooting gallery' was swept to the ground with a bang as our hero crash-landed onto the sitting room floor. Lights went on in every window in the house but the helpers outside decided not to wait on the post-mortem.

Hollywood Connections

Although not widely acknowledged, Borrisokane has two major connections with the film industry.

Reginald Ingram Hitchcock
1893 - 1950

Reginald Ingram Hitchcock (who later shortened his name to Rex Ingram) was the son of Reverend Francis Hitchcock, the local Church of Ireland rector and he spent much of his childhood years at the Glebe House in Borrisokane. At the age of 18, after the death of his mother, he headed to the east coast of America. He was to go on to become known as the 'Master of Silent Cinema' and was a huge influence on the growth and development of the film industry. His father, Reverend Hitchcock was a colourful character by all accounts of his time in Borris before being moved to Kinnity on promotion. Reverend Hitchcock had a love of sport and the outdoor life. He wrote several novels and was a noted boxer in his younger days. He became very good friends with the local parish priest, his near neighbour, Father John Meagher and the pair would good out shooting crows together every week, bringing young Rex along with them. Both of these clergymen were soon to be asked to become the first trustees of the proposed new hall to be bequeathed by the Clarke family.

In his later years, in an article in the *London Daily Express*, Rex Ingram described himself thus;

> 'I am a fatalist, because it keeps me from worrying,
> I am superstitious, perhaps because I'm Irish,
> Good omens encourage me and bad ones
> I can avert by crossing my fingers and spitting.
> This I learned at the age of eight years
> from the parish priest of Borrisokane, Co. Tipperary.
> It has yet to fail me!'

Growing up in Borris, Rex grew to love the sporting country life. He and his brother Frank along with their Irish water spaniel 'Towser' would have been a common sight along the marsh by the riverbank at the turn of the last century. All of this influenced and shaped his belief (long ahead of his time) that films should be shot outdoors 'on location', contrary to the views then held by the established studio bosses. He was a regular visitor to Leap Castle, once the seat of the O'Carroll clan and by reputation still the most haunted castle in Ireland.

He was educated at St Columba's College, Rathfarnham, Dublin. He was fond of sport but it was only after an accident on the playing fields of St Columba's that his artistic leanings were encouraged by a teacher, Mr Gwynn. He left Ireland for New York at the age of 18 years in 1911. He was destined never to return. He found work as a clerk in a railway stockyard and studied sculpture at Yale University, but shortly after this came his 'light bulb moment.' A chance meeting with the son of inventor Thomas Edison (who was a pioneer in film) gave him a start in the industry. He became an actor – in the then silent movies – at Edison Studios, New York, going on from there to become a successful screenwriter for Fox Films having shortened his name to Rex Ingram. At the age of 23 he directed his first film for the Universal Film Company. He teamed up with D.W. Griffith and Erich Von Stroheim and this trio went on to become the most powerful force in the industry at the time. He discovered and directed such early stars as Rudolph Valentino, Ramon Novarro and Alice Terry (whom he later married).

The much loved and lusted Rudolph Valentino died at the age of 31 in 1926 to the inconsolable grief of women all over the Western world. The circumstances of his death were dramatic and mystery still surrounds the identity of the mysterious lady in black who placed white flowers on his fresh grave. There is remarkable archive film footage of his coffin being borne from St Patrick's Cathedral, New York and bearing his coffin are two instantly recognizable film stars, Charlie Chaplin and Rex Ingram. His most notable films were:

Under Crimson Skies (1920), **The Four Horsemen of the Apocalypse** (1921), **The Prisoner of Zenda** (1922), **Scaramouch** (1923), **Mare Nostrum** (1926) **The Garden of Allah** (1927) and his last film, **Baroud** (1933) a 'talkie' filmed in Morocco, in which he played the lead role, but sadly not his best film.

In 1924 after a falling out with W.B. Meyer of MGM over the production of **Ben-Hur**, he departed to set up his own studios in Nice, France which are today known as the Victorine Studios. In 1934 the Ingrams went to Egypt to where they returned after the war to retrieve their art collection from the Cairo Museum. He was decorated in later life by the French Government. He is described in James Joyce's masterpiece **Ulysses** as 'Rex Ingram ~ Pageant Master'. He was also a talented sculptor and artist, these pursuits he followed until his death in Los Angeles in 1950. His wife Alice died in 1987. His huge influence on and legacy to film in the 20th century are indelible, as one of the first of a wave of great European film directors who shaped and dominated Hollywood.

Martin Sheen

A more recent Hollywood connection is that of pacifist and activist, actor Martin Sheen, now an Irish citizen. Possibly best known the world over for his portrayal of Josiah Bartlet in the famous TV series *The West Wing*, for which he has won a Golden Globe.

Born Ramon Esteves in 1940 in Dayton, Ohio, his stage name became Martin Sheen (after the Bishop of New York, Fulton Sheen). Martin's mother, Mary Ann Phelan came from Tower Hill (now Patsy Reddan's pub) and his uncle Bob Phelan was one of the town's great characters. His first cousin is the well known Sean 'Scrapper ' Phelan of Mill Street, as good a hurler as ever stood between the posts minding the net for Borris. A number of the Esteves family were christened in St Peter & Paul's church on Mill Street. Even as a young child

Martin could strongly identify with the characters in the movies and he always wanted to become an actor.

After winning a trip as first prize in an acting competition, he went to New York in 1959 and spent ten years there in theatre. His first big break on Broadway came in a play called *The Subject was Roses* which went on tour and was finally made into a film. He went on to achieve widespread recognition both on TV and Broadway before starring in such films as *The Incident* (1967), *Catch 22* (1970) and *Badlands* (1973) alongside Sissy Spacek in the director Terence Malick's debut film. The latter film was based on the true story of Charles Starkweather, who in an apparent fixation on movie actor James Dean, went on a killing spree with his girlfriend killing ten people including her parents in 1958. Bruce Springsteen's song 'Nebraska' was inspired by this violent episode. In the film, Sheen was considered something of a James Dean look-alike, blazing a trail of destruction across America's badlands in the 1950s. He has said many times that he considers *Badlands* to be his best film.

Sheen gave a brilliant performance in the definitive Vietnam war movie of all time, *Apocalypse Now* (1979). This film focused on the same themes of war and peace, good and evil, encountered on a journey as had previously been explored in Joseph Conrad's novel *Heart of Darkness*. Sheen plays the role of a young US army captain, Willard, on an odyssey up a Cambodian river in search of the mad maverick Colonel Kurtz played by Marlon Brando. Kurtz had gone 'native', developed an understanding with the Viet Cong enemy and had carved out his patch in the jungle according to his own rules. He had a penchant for beheading enemies and friends. Williard was given the unenviable mission to 'terminate with extreme prejudice' the warlord Kurtz. He delivers a memorable performance of burning intensity as he witnesses and eventually succumbs to the madness around him. He strikes such empathy that we see the experience through his eyes and from his perspective. The film, shot in the Philippines during the Marcos regime, was originally five to seven hours long, so the pruning shears had to be applied to bring it to a commercial two and a half hours. It was highly ambitious, trying to bring in all the issues in the book and overloaded with cross reference to various authors and themes. Sheen suffered a heart attack on set but his younger brother Joe Estevez stood in for him in long shots and for some voice overs. But it was a financial disaster (reaching costs of $30M against a budget of $12M) rendering the producer Francis Ford Coppola almost bankrupt. However, it has not dated and remains the best war film ever made. The dramatic use of sound alone is brilliant, particularly in early scenes like the helicopter attack. For this writer seeing a military helicopter or listening to Billy Joel's classic performance of 'Goodnight Saigon,' still evokes the powerful defining images of *Apocalypse Now*.

Performing in Hugh Leonard's *Da* in 1988 he insisted that the town of his spiritual roots get a mention in the film. Although the line "You wouldn't have a grope with the typist from Borrisokane" is hardly the stuff of cinematic history, he was granted his wish.

His sons are the actors Emilio Estevez and Charlie Sheen and he appeared with the latter in **Wall Street** (1987). He was and is a frequent visitor to his many Borris cousins particularly Teresa Bourke of Kilbarron. After finishing **The West Wing** in 2006, he studied at NUI Galway. He completed a full semester and was conferred with an honorary arts doctorate by the National University of Ireland. When approached that same year to be asked if he would consider playing a part in the proposed film adaptation of **Stella Days**, his response was characteristic and instant; 'I would do anything for Borrisokane.'

For this writer, meeting Martin Sheen (on the set of **Da** in Bray) was a most pleasant and memorable experience. For a man who has achieved such widespread deserved acclaim he comes across as an affable easy going family guy, ever keen to discuss his North Tipperary roots. He gives the impression that he would probably be just as much at home in Hannigan's pub in Kilbarron or in Yank's in Borris as anywhere in the world.

CINEMA IN THE FIFTIES

HOLLYWOOD – THE BIG PICTURE

The 50th anniversary of the birth of cinema was a time of great change in the film industry world-wide. This was particularly true in America, which accounted for most of the global market for Western cinema. The industry's infrastructure was massive, with mammoth studios, such as Universal City in Los Angeles, the first to arrive (in 1912) with its back lot of 420 acres and 28 stage sets. Paramount had arrived a month later, soon to be followed by 20th Century Fox, Warner Brothers, RKO and Metro-Goldwyn-Mayer (MGM). Hollywood was big business in every respect. That large old wooden 'Hollywood' sign in the hills overlooking the Mecca of world film is a constant in the mind's eye.

The financial rewards were staggering in a cut-throat business but it was not necessarily the actors who benefited in the structural hierarchy. In this harsh environment, black and Latino actors faced prejudice and being gay or indeed a single parent was fatal to a career. Socially, it manufactured people in terms of creating big names for consumption and ultimately disposed of them, as yesterday's 'child star' became today's unwanted actor. The Oscars – as the Academy Awards became known – were intended as a gesture by Hollywood's artists to honour achievement in the industry. They had grown out of all proportion, to become the biggest media circus in the land. The fad of the 'drive-in' movies, reflecting the American obsession with both cars and films, was at its peak. It had been the ultimate teenage dating ritual but was itself becoming dated by the end of the decade.

In balance sheet terms, the industry's problems became as fundamental as rising production overheads combined with diminishing audiences. The industry's absolute peak year had been 1946 with a staggering 90 million admissions per week. From then on it was steady decline. Hollywood's golden era had lasted from 1935 to 1955, but now its traditional studio system of film production and distribution was under threat, both from European films and smaller independent film makers. The number of independently produced films doubled annually and successful directors were being 'discovered' to high acclaim. If films were to be commercially successful and make more money then the studios would have to make changes. There were ongoing technical innovations in colour filming which by the mid-50s had increased to more than half of all films made world-wide. Technicolor's traditional dominance was threatened by smaller newcomers like Eastman who had successfully introduced the Kodachrome single strip colour film known as Eastman-Color in 1952. Paramount's Vistavision was used for the first time in *White Christmas* (1954). A refined system known as the Todd-AO process was used to good effect in the highly successful *Around the World in Eighty Days* (1956) featuring David Niven and a host of stars. Walt Disney's cinemascope production of the delightful *Lady and The Tramp* (1955) combined adventure, music and comedy with the voice of Peggy Lee as a siamese cat. *Dangerous When Wet* (1953) features a delightful underwater sequence when heroine Esther Williams swims alongside 'Tom and Jerry'. But despite these technical improvements in colour and quality, the proliferation of television, which first appeared in the 1930's, was the single biggest threat. The film industry almost collapsed before the domestic comfort of fireside television, as the small screens spread across the homes of America. From 28% of households in 1950 it grew to 89% by 1959. The initial reaction of the big studios was to place an embargo on old films being rerun on television. They even had a ban on their contracted film stars from making TV appearances which was only lifted in 1956. But by way of fight back, many new techniques and special effects were tried. Some of these such as wide-screen and stereo have remained with us in one form or another, whilst others were mere gimmicks.

Swords & Sandals

A major innovation of the time was Cinemascope – a wide-screen process first developed in the 1920's by a Frenchman Henri Jacques Chrétien, whereby for the first time standard 35 mm film could be 'stretched' to produce a wide screen image giving the familiar letterbox shape 2 1/2 times its height. This was a success and a godsend to the industry as they could now show both cause and effect in one shot.

The first film made in Cinemascope by Fox was *The Robe* first shown at the Roxy Theatre in New York in 1953. This was about a Roman centurion (Richard Burton) ordered to crucify the Messiah (whose face was never shown in the film), and his conversion to Christianity when he donned the robe. It also starred Victor Mature and Jean Simmons. There are various urban myths surrounding these films, particularly the yarn about the red mini car appearing in the background in the chariot race but this writer has never witnessed any of them through many viewings.

It was soon followed by Cecil B. De Mille's *The Ten Commandments* and M.G.M's *Ben-Hur*, both shot in the same spectacular mould. *Ben-Hur* was a film of four hours running time, based on a novel written in

1880 by Lew Wallace. It was the most expensive film ever made but it was also a massive commercial success for MGM. It picked up 12 Academy Awards. **Quo Vadis** was typical of the genre. Three hours long, with only Peter Ustinov's splendidly daft and camp Nero to relieve the tedium for which he earned a Golden Globe award. At the time, the parting of the Red Sea by Moses (Charlton Heston) in **The Ten Commandments** was the most innovative spectacle on film. A total of 300,000 gallons of water was used for this scene alone. Despite all that water, you might notice that the Israelites make it across – on dry ground? A Hollywood miracle!

Further epics with massively inflated budgets such as **Helen of Troy, Solomon and Sheeba** and **Cleopatra** were to follow, but – with the possible exception of **Spartacus** – the genre began to lose its appeal to the public. Howard Hawks abandoned the genre to go back to Westerns after the spectacular failure of his Egyptian epic **Land of the Pharaohs**. The scale, colour and a cast of thousands could not hide mediocre acting and long drawn out plots. Even Spartacus had its cringeworthy moments such as his lieutenant running in and almost genuflecting announces 'Spartacus, Spartacus, I will follow you to the ends of the earth', all delivered in a South Bronx accent. Audiences grew tired of biblical characters, men decked out in leather skirts complete with modern haircuts and American accents which had limited credibility with the local audience.

A whole new trend was to move far away from the studios to exotic locations world-wide, where films in a natural outdoor setting could be made far cheaper than in studio. 20th Century Fox continued this trend with the musical **South Pacific** which was shot on location in Northern Ibiza. Because of the availability of cheap labour and wonderful background, Rome was the favourite destination for American producers. In other cases films became synonymous with cities such as **Love is a Many Splendid Thing** (Hong Kong), **Summertime** (Venice), **Roman Holiday** and **Three Coins in the Fountain** (Rome). **Roman Holiday**, a comedy starring Gregory Peck and Audrey Hepburn was also hugely influential in creating a world wide fashion icon out of the Roman's favourite mode of transport, the Vespa motorcycle. **Around The World In Eighty Days** became the ultimate geography flick. Considered chic and innovative at the time, it is now passé. In **Love in the Afternoon**, the director Billy Wilder decided to send the whole cast and crew to an exotic island just off Jamaica to complete the outdoor sequences. The liquor was cheap and the hospitality was extremely generous giving rise to an inordinate delay in completion of the film which the financiers could not fathom. Eventually an urgent telegraph arrived on the island from the films financial backers at home in America:

'Finalise immediately ... The costs are staggering.

The response was swift : 'So are the cast.'

There were similar problems (but inverse results) with the shooting of **The African Queen** in the Belgian Congo. The whole cast and crew fell ill to a strange infection, rapidly shedding pounds in the process. They carried on with just two, John Huston the director and Humphrey Bogart, one of the stars, staying healthy. The cause of the virus was eventually discovered to be the Lake Victoria drinking water and these two gentlemen were immune because they only drank whiskey, which surely inoculated a leech infested Bogart as he pulled the tug-boat through the jungle mire.

There were various experimental techniques such as three dimensional films which had to be viewed through special green and red spectacles distributed in the cinemas. The first 3-D film with stereophonic sound was *House of Wax* (1953) in which a number of objects were effectively hurled at the audience. Ironically, the director Andre De Toth had just one eye so he probably never came to fully appreciate his own 3-D effects. However the audience who were being asked to wear masks with one red eye and one green eye on their night out found the viewing tiresome in the extreme.

In addition to vision and sound, Hollywood even tried to add another sense, that of smell to the cinema experience with AromoRama and Glorious-Smell-O-Visions. *In Behind The Great Wall* (1959) the scent of smoke, incense, orange peel and burning pitch were included in a total of 27 different smells emanating from the cinema. Unfortunately the 'smellies' as they came to be known, were not successful for a number of practical reasons. One of these was that the scent of a previous film tended to linger on in the cinema resulting in people who had just taken their seats looking at each other suspiciously as the possible source of the smell.

Perhaps the most bizarre gimmick of all came from eccentric B-movie director William Castle in his 1959 thriller *The Tingler*. He had tiny electric motors placed under the seats and at key moments in the film the audience were 'shocked' by electric currents. Hard to see Slevin Electrical agreeing to wire up the Stella for such a novel effect.

Possibly in another reaction to TV, Hollywood began to attract a new audience by showing controversial or adult topics deemed unsuitable for family viewing. Ida Lupina's *Outrage* (1950) caused an uproar at the time because the subject matter was rape. Ida Lupina was an extraordinary character not least because she broke through the 'glass ceiling' of a male dominated industry. After early appearances in *High Sierra* (1941) and opposite Humphrey Bogart in *They Drive by Night* (1943) she proved she had brains as well as beauty to become a freelance actress, then writer and finally a successful director. The film *The Moon is Blue* (1954) a risqué sex comedy which although harmless by today's standards then broke new ground in terms of permissiveness. It was released without a seal of approval from the established watchdog of the time, the Production Code. The mention of the words 'virgin' and 'seduce' meant that it that did not comply with the code of conduct and therefore did not receive widespread showing. It set the scene for the release of Elia Kazan's *Baby Doll* (1956), a somewhat comic take on the theme of sexual repression. Similarly, *Picnic* (1955) was ahead of its time, with female temperatures rising when William Holden removes his starched shirt.

In *The Defiant Ones* (1958) director Stanley Kramer tackled racism. It featured the animosity between a black convict (Sidney Poitier) and a white convict (Tony Curtis) shackled together. Controversial enough in its day. Romantic films aimed at a female audience were popular with a trend to remake 1930's 'weepies', best exemplified by Douglas Sirk's Technicolor operas *Magnificent Obsession* (1954) and *All That Heaven Allows* (1953). *The Company She Keeps* (1951) was a mild banal drama now noteworthy for only one aspect and that is the very first (uncredited) film appearance of the great Jeff Bridges, as a toddler.

The decade brought us some great supporting actors who although never hogged the limelight nonetheless brought great presence to films of the era. One such actor was Karl Malden (above) whose craggy face and big nose became known and loved in films such as *Halls of Montezuma* (1951), *Fear Strikes Out* (1957), *On the Waterfront* (1953) and *A Streetcar Named Desire* (1951).

The 1950s saw the first steps towards the globalization

of popular culture and that culture was American. Rock & Roll music was all the rage and Hollywood was quick to capitalise on the latest trends in popular music. The forerunners were Elvis Presley's early films *Love Me Tender* (1956), *Loving You* (1956), and *Jailhouse Rock* (1957), the first of 33 films he would make. Although not critically acclaimed, they proved a good vehicle for his brilliant musical talent. These along with *The Blackboard Jungle* (1955) and Bill Haley's *Rock Around the Clock* (1959) were cloned by a host of teenage beach movies.

By 1958 it was estimated that most of Hollywood's films were being made independently for audiences in the 18 to 30 age bracket, leading to a spate of exploitative teenage B-movies – now best forgotten – such as *Sorority Girl* (1957), *Runaway Daughters* (1957), *The Cool and the Crazy* (1958), *Daddy-O* (1959). This was to have its own impact on film scores over time. However what the public demanded were 'stars'.

There is an argument that American youth culture began in the 50s with stars such as Marilyn Monroe, a brilliant comedienne who led a chaotic private life. She replaced Ava Gardner as MGM's screen goddess of the decade. She became the major female star of the 50s after early success with Bette Davis in *All About Eve* (1950), *Let's Make It Legal* (1951), *Clash by Night* (1952), *How To Marry A Millionaire* (1955) and *Niagara* (1953). But the era of the studios control over contracted actors had not yet ended. Marilyn had signed a 'slave' contract with 20th Century Fox in 1950. This stipulated that she would work exclusively for that

studio and tied her a set wage of $3500 a week regardless
of box office numbers. This contrasted with Jane Russell
her co-star in the musical ***Gentlemen Prefer Blondes***
(1952) who was paid $150,000 for her role. However
the brunette and the blonde became great friends. In
1953 they both made their respective imprints together
in the wet cement outside the legendary Grauman's
Chinese Theatre Hollywood Boulevard. Monroe proved
to be a shrewd businesswoman and after a protracted
legal battle 20th Century Fox finally capitulated.
The image of a subway train blowing a gust of air up
Marilyn's skirt in the ***Seven Year Itch*** (1955) remains
a defining and iconic image in Hollywood's history.
She teamed up with Britain's most esteemed actor, the
legendary Laurence Olivier (who also was a producer)
in ***The Prince and the Showgirl*** (1957). She went on
to make one of the best comedies of the 50s alongside
Jack Lemmon and Tony Curtis indulging in a bit of
cross-dressing in ***Some Like it Hot*** (1959). In order to
accentuate her 'sexy' walk for this film, Monroe had a

quarter inch taken off the right heel of her shoes. In recent times this film has been acclaimed by a panel of film experts as the funniest film ever made. Eminent film critic Ron Corbet considers the closing dialogue in *Some Like it Hot* as the very pinnacle of Hollywood comedy – so here you go:

As they escape in the motorboat driven by love lorn Osgood (Joe E. Brown) he proposes to Daphne (Jack Lemmon)

Daphne: Well, in the first place, I'm not a natural blonde.

Osgood: Doesn't matter.

Daphne: I smoke! I smoke all the time.

Osgood: I don't care

Daphne: I've a terrible past and for three years now I've been living with a saxophone player.

Osgood: I forgive you.

Daphne: I can never have children.

Osgood: We can adopt some

Daphne: You don't understand Osgood! I'm a man.
Osgood: Well ... nobody's perfect!

It appears she was used and abused both on and off screen and once poignantly claimed, 'I know that men don't see me, they just lay eyes on me.' Marilyn Monroe died tragically in 1962 in dramatic circumstances that to this day are the cause of intense speculation. She remains an immortal icon in film history.

The development of Cinerama was considered a revolutionary new system in its day. It initially involved showing film via three projectors each aligned to show 1/3 of the film on a large curved screen creating an illusion of vastness. The first documentary shown using this technique was *This is Cinerama* (1952) which gave the audience the sensation of riding on a roller-coaster. The first Cinerama cinema in Ireland was The Plaza, Granby Row, Dublin. The most notable feature film in this medium was the overly long *How the West was Won* which bored the doors off a busload of Borrisokane school-kids on their annual school tour. *Lady And The Tramp* (1955) was the first animated feature to use the Cinerama format and remains a classic in that it has stood the test of time. In the long run, Cinerama was not helped by the choice of films available such as *Seven Brides for Seven Brothers* or the truly awful *It's a Mad Mad Mad Mad World* which duly bombed at the box office. Appropriate perhaps that the Plaza eventually morphed into Ireland's first wax museum. The whole process was eventually abandoned in favour of a single-lens 70mm process.

In any event, by 1955 Hollywood was facing a

different threat – politics. Its very existence was under attack from Senator Joe McCarthy's paranoid anti-Communist witch-hunt which had resumed from where it took off in the previous decade. His aide was one Richard Nixon (yes him). There was a genuine fear at the time that Communists were taking over the whole motion picture business and actors, directors, writers and producers were summoned to appear before the House un-American Activities committee. That was not a fun gig. Even established stalwarts like Cecil B. DeMille got in on the act. He went to the trouble of forming his own organization with the grandiose title of 'The Cecil B. DeMille Foundation for Political Freedom', urging actors to join and unite in the face of socialism. The profession was split down the middle, with directors like John Huston counter-punching by forming his Committee for the First Amendment. There were unbelievable scenes as actors, producers and directors denounced each other as Communists on the flimsiest of evidence in order to save their own careers. Being pro-union was considered enough to be branded a Communist. The question always posed at a court martial type public hearing was:

'Are you, or have you ever been a member of the Communist party?' Many of Hollywood's biggest names were blacklisted and some of the screenwriters had to write under false names to earn a livelihood. The playwright Arthur Miller could have had his scheduled appearance before the committee culled if he acceded to the chairman's wish to be photographed with his new wife Marilyn Monroe. They were known as the 'Owl and the Pussy Cat'. Miller did not respond.

Stars like Burt Lancaster found themselves being hounded by the FBI for years afterwards. As the process never outed a single Red of any significance, people began to tire of McCarthy and his hysteria. He went on to accuse a decorated war hero of being a communist and after this unsavory episode his committee was dissolved. McCarthy himself died soon afterwards as a result of chronic alcoholism.

Another big change towards the end of the era was the easing of the Production Code or the Hays Code. These were rigid rules about what could be shown or could not, originally set down in the 1930s. The 'League of Decency' was still quite powerful in America around this period. This was a Catholic lobby group backed by Protestant and Jewish interests who would 'vet' each film for scenes depicting either sex or violence. Films were rated accordingly, the most feared grade being branded a capital C which meant forbidden viewing for all Catholics. Unhindered by American film laws, in France, Roger Vadim shot **And God Created Woman** (1956) mainly to point his camera at a very young Brigitte Bardot scantily clad along St Tropez beach. But many films accurately portrayed Hollywood as a cruel alien environment. **The Bad And The Beautiful** (1952) featuring Kirk Douglas and Lana Turner was a case in point. Here we had Hollywood portraying itself in all its cynicism, ruthlessness and exploitation. It was entirely appropriate that Douglas (of the famous trademark dimple on his chin) became the first actor to break the system of the seven year contracts. These had bound stars to work for one studio with no say in the choice of roles they were given. He walked out on Paramount and formed his own company Bryna Productions. But for all the various difficulties and challenges, the stars of the time managed to maintain something of an aura about themselves, rare today with celebrity coverage at saturation point. Cary Grant, a byword for suave good lucks and the smoothest of screen talents tried to keep his age a secret. He had good reason. When the actor (born in 1904 ... now it can be told) starred in most of his suave playboy roles in films such as *Indiscreet* (1958) he was into his mid 50s! A curious journalist once sent a telegram to his agent enquiring:

'How old ... Cary Grant?'
The star himself replied: 'Old Cary Grant just fine. How you?'

And what more can we say about the immortal Cary Grant? He has had such a long, brilliant career and made so many films that even confining him to the 1950s is insufficient. We could talk about his role as a gynecologist in *People Will Talk* (1951) under the skillful direction of the great Joe Mankiewicz. But perhaps his defining 1950s role was in *An Affair to Remember* (1957) as a playboy aboard an ocean liner who falls in love with a singer (played by Deborah Kerr) when they are both engaged to other people. The man was 53 years old (not that you'd notice) and the lady was 35. Written and skillfully directed by Leo McCarey, they agree to meet six months later – but only if they still feel the same way – at the Empire State Building. Just watch it and ladies keep the hanky ready. By the way, the same Empire State Building is the structural star of over 250 films.

Then, as now, love affairs between actors provided fodder for gossip columnists. Katherine Hepburn and Spencer Tracy had an affair lasting a full 27 years. This was reflected in their nine film appearances together.

Other introspective films with bitchy tales of ambition and betrayal of the era included *In a Lonely Place* (1950), *All About Eve* (1950), and *The Barefoot Contessa* (1954). Billy Wilder, who directed some of the bleakest Hollywood films ever, produced *Sunset Boulevard* (1950). Veteran actress Gloria Swanson plays a faded old movie queen (herself) alongside William Holden as a young ambitious screenwriter. In the film, they first meet in Swanson's old mansion where the gaunt old butler is played by the legendary film director Erich Von Stroheim, ironically the first victim of Hollywood's notorious studio system. Holden casually greets her with the laconic remark.

'You're Norma Desmond ... You used to be big in the silent pictures.'

Swanson proudly stiffens up to deliver the famous response.

'I am big! It's the pictures that got small.'

Cowboys

The romance of the American 'Wild West' gripped the public imagination like nothing before or since. The concept of the lone cowboy riding across daunting plains, under massive skies, clearly represented the struggle of the individual against all the odds. Truly the stuff and essence of the American dream. Some of the best westerns ever were made in the 1950's. Cowboy films were undoubtedly the big hit at the Stella but the Westerner was a folk hero long before cinema. In rural Ireland, the culture and trappings of the Cowboys were well embedded thanks to popular books. The novels of Zane Gray and the Smith & Street Western magazines were amongst the most popular reading material in rural Ireland. The two best read were *The Lone Star Ranger* and *Robbery Under Arms*. Indeed cowboys from 30s films had trickled into consciousness even without cinema, as most people had heard of Tom Mix, Hopalong Cassidy and the gloriously titled Lash LaRue. Then of course there were the singing cowboys such as Tex Ritter, Gene Autrey and Roy Rogers, who, with his horse 'Trigger' was such a big hit on his visits to Dublin. The classic hombre portrayed was typically a laconic slow moving character, usually trying to distance himself from a violent past. Slow to anger, he would become explosive when called into action. Everybody had thought he was mean but when he dispensed with the real 'baddies' in the end he became the town's own hero. One feature of cowboy films was the absence of meaningful dialogue. This is exemplified by the survival of such mundane lines as 'Take 'em to Missouri' from **Red River**. What marked out a true cowboy was not necessarily his skill on a horse or with a gun. Lack of these attributes never troubled a clearly overweight and unfit John Wayne. His strengths were not athletic but he had the knack of being able to 'walk tall' and his body language implied he would take no nonsense from anybody. He was superstitious. In each cowboy film, he always carried the same pair of six-guns which he had first used in **The Big Trail** (1930).

What marked out a true hombre was his table manners or indeed the lack of same. When a real cowboy walked into a saloon, he strode manfully up to the counter, oblivious of all the attention he was receiving from the imbibing low-lifers in the background. He ordered a neat whiskey which meant a big bottle and a glass. If the bartender could slide them along the surface for the length of the counter then all the better. He filled the glass with a flick of his wrist and emptied it with one jerk of his head and a gulp. Nobody in Ireland drank whiskey like this. They had more respect for whiskey. If that stuff had half the strength of Jamesion or Paddy, he would surely have buckled at the knees. But no trouble to our cowboy. If he wasn't in the mood for shooting undesirables there and then, he would amble to a lone table with bottle in hand, sure of the attentions of the card school or the dancing girl. A class act, surely a desperado or even 'Marlboro Man'.

The era began with Gregory Peck winning the title 'Cowboy Star of the Year' (over John Wayne) for his role in *The Gunfighter* (1950). The best of Cowboy films continued to roll out in the 50s, featuring established stars from the 40s such as John Wayne, Gary Cooper, Joel McCrea, Randolph Scott, and James Stewart. Although based on a short span of American history (1865 - 1890) the genre proved so popular that Hollywood mass produced Westerns. This resulted in very many films of poor quality, repetitive story-lines and bad acting. These have not stood the test of time. But there were notable exceptions. For many the era kicked in with *Winchester 73* as James Stewart (revealing a mean streak at last) beats up veteran Western hero Dan Durea. Whilst many classic cowboy films were made, including *Rio Bravo*, *Shane*, *The Big Country*, *The Searchers*, *Commanche* and *High Noon*. In some cases the real star was the horse. Whilst Monument Valley made a spectacular backdrop, the 'action' was often of the wallpaper variety and not exactly an assault on the senses that would have been expected from the title.

However, regardless of quality, an abundance of films with such lyrically evocative if somewhat macho titles as *Arrow in the Dust, The First Texan, A Man without a Star, Band of the River, Man with the Gun, The Gunfight at Dodge City, Showdown at Abeline, Rancho Notorious, Saddle Tramp, Johnny Guitar, The Sheriff of Fractured Jaw, The Naked Spur, The Left Handed Gun, Only the Valiant, Broken Lance, Seven Men From Now, Silver Lode, The Furies, Springfield, Rifle, The Tall T, The Gunfighter, Face of a Fugitive, The Fastest Gun Alive, Dragoon Wells Massacre, Blood on the Moon, Dakota Incident, Dallas, Ride Lonesome, Saddle the Wind, Wagonmaster, Seventh Cavalry, The Yellow Mountain, The Law and Jake Wade, Warlock,* or *Last Train to Gun Hill* were a sure-fire draw at the Stella. It was expected that these would at least meet with the trades description act and do what it stated in the title.

A local criticism of some Western B-movies was the lack of Indians. With pulsating music in the build up, expectations were always going to be high, so having the same half dozen Apaches being recycled in the finale was never going to wash with the demanding Stella audience. As for shooting locks off doors – it's just not possible – only in Cowboy films, stupid! Younger cowboy fans were less critical. For them, Sitting Bull, Crazy Horse and The Battle of the Little Big Horn had decidedly more appeal than the historic battles of the

Boyne, Clontarf and Aughrim put together. Such was their love of the Cowboys, that they were more than happy to overlook the obvious flaws.

The 'Cowboys' in the Stella usually involved full audience participation. Could anything have been more exciting than John Wayne riding directly into an Apache ambush. Managing to beat off most of his attackers single handed, the scene closes on a wounded Apache with just enough strength left to aim his rifle at our hero's back. The full front row of youngsters stand and shout a warning. Too late ... Bang! ... The big fella is winged and goes down. The Apache (obviously feeling better now) reloads. Wayne recovers 'Jays', he was only pretending.

'Yippeee,' 50 bloodthirsty young voices yell out from the front row. 'Get him, Hondo ... Finish him off!'

None of your Roy Rogers here, be the herrings! Shooting Indians in the hand, making up and riding off into the sunset singing. Nope, this was the Duke.

The Western was the favourite genre of prolific director John Ford, who made over 200 films including 80 war documentaries. He was an amazing character. An eccentric Irish-American, he suffered from bad eyesight, a hot temper and a funeral thirst for drink. In World War 2 he joined the US navy and was actually injured as he filmed the ***Battle of Midway***. He went on to make a string of classics including ***Fort Apache, Red River, My Darling Clementine, She wore a Yellow Ribbon, Rio Grande,*** and ***The Searchers***. More than any other director, he identified with the awe inspiring backdrop of Colorado's Monument Valley which had been the setting for so many of Zane Grey's classic novels. For spectacle combined with action there was no natural setting quite so suited to making Westerns. The dome like cliffs were ideal, with seemingly just one really spectacular gap or 'pass' between the mountains. 'Cut 'em off at the pass' never had such urgency before. Ford arrived there in 1939 for the making of **Stagecoach** the doyen of Westerns, providing badly needed work for the local Navajo Indians. He loved to relate the tale of how he hired the local medicine man to ensure he got the right weather conditions for filming. Usually he was never let down, until one day a downpour began when the medicine man had forecasted sunshine. When asked why, his reply was simply that his radio was broken! He won four Academy Awards and died aged 80, in 1973.

We kids developed a good working knowledge of the various Indian tribes via Hollywood. There were Commanches, Cheyenne, Choctaws, Cherokees, Dakotas, Lakotas, Pawnees, Shawnees, but the tribe described as a great nation (mainly by themselves) were the Sioux. Most feared of all were the Apaches, who in dress were a bit more like the cowboys (except for long black flowing hair) and they used rifles while riding bareback. The poor old Indians were portrayed as primitive savages, the only 'good' one being the proverbial 'dead' one in the words of hardened cowpokes. When an Indian was shot dead, it did not seem to be a big issue, as it happened with recurring frequency and they were cannon fodder anyway. When a cowboy died, it was, more often than not that we, the audience, had got to know his character beforehand and could relate to him. The action would slow momentarily for his last words against a poignant background of sad music. Then a glance backwards towards a lonely grave of stones marked with a little wooden cross. Meanwhile, the vultures would circle and polish off the remains of the unloved Indians. The Indians themselves were never referred to as Native Americans and finally began to earn some respect in films like *Broken Arrow* (1950) and *Apache* (1954). The latter film featured Burt Lancaster in the title role looking something like Granny Reilly on a bad hair day. We learned about and empathised with the outlaws such as Billy the Kid, Frank and Jessie James, Butch Cassidy, Black Bart and Wild Bill Hitchcock. We were later to learn that many of these outlaws were of Irish ethnic origin. We knew more of the history of the American civil war between the Confederates and the Yankees than we did of the Irish civil war which was airbrushed from history.

There was a long queue to see *The Beast of Hollow Mountain* (1956) which was a kind of cross between a horror and a western. There was to be disappointment, as the 'Beast' turned out to be a lizard ridiculously magnified with slow awkward body movements. More comic than scary.

MUSIC

And then of course there was the music, (or the film score as we later learned as its proper description) which was a major part in the overall experience and nowhere more so than with the Cowboys. The real significance of the impact of music usually came near the climax of the action when the wagon train was being attacked by Indians. Just as the first wagon went ablaze and things were looking grim, the familiar sound of a distant bugle sounding reveille signalled the imminent arrival of the Seventh Cavalry who would soon rout the invaders to the cheers of the young audience. But prior to that experience, from sitting on our Mammy's knees we knew the songs:

'Robin Hood, Robin Hood, riding through the glen,
Robin Hood, Robin Hood with his band of men,

Feared by the bad,
Loved by the good,
Robin Hood ... Robin Hood ... Robin Hood.'

There were similar upbeat songs about Tom Dooley, Davy Crockett and sad sentimental songs like 'Bridle Hanging on the Wall'. We had the redoubtable duo, Laurel and Hardy *Way Out West* in cowboy territory this time:

'In the Blue Ridge mountains of Virginia,
  On the trail of the lonesome pine'

The definitive cowboy song of the era had to be:

'South of the Border ... down Mexico way.
That's where I fell in love
when stars came out to play'

For early geography we had:

'North to Alaska, up North the rush is on,
Way up North ... way up North'

The classic song Mona Lisa was first a hit in *Captain Carey U.S.A.* (1950) sung by a blind Italian street singer or for real class, how about Mario Lanza (as a GI) singing *'Because You're Mine'* from the 1952 film of the same name.

And always 'High Hopes' from *A Hole in the Head* (1959) featuring Old Blue Eyes Frank Sinatra or mild romance from Doris Day, with the song 'By the Light of the Silvery Moon' or better still singing 'Que Sera Sera' in *The Man Who Knew Too Much* (1956)

Not to mention Grace Kelly and Bing Crosby singing 'True Love' in *High Society* (1956) or for sheer pathos, Tex Ritter singing: 'Do not forsake me oh my dahling on this our wedding day'

As the apathetic townspeople started to 'chicken' leaving a grim Gary Cooper to face music of a different variety in *High Noon*. The sheriff had foolishly postponed two major life events, his engagement and his retirement, in view of the impending prospect of a third, his death. The pained look on Cooper's face was no act, as he was suffering from a burst ulcer while shooting. At the Oscars that year the film won Best Actor, Best Score, and Best Song. It was apparently (yet another) a metaphor for the way the American public stood idly by during the McCarthy witch-hunt.

That said, many people throughout Ireland would have experienced similar feelings of isolation when they tried to create initiatives in demoralised communities. Now a catchy song which identified with a particular film was particularly appealing. Alternatively, when the whole film was built around the music, giving rise to musicals with a raft of songs such as *Showboat, Guys and Dolls, Singing in the Rain* or the western musical *Oklahoma* (where not a single shot was fired in anger) the end result was abject boredom amongst the kids. To have to sit through song after song from the likes of Curley the Cowboy about 'cattle all standing like statues' with not an 'injun' in sight was all too much.

The best of the era's musicals were in the early 50s. On the advice of his costume designer, Yul Brynner shaved all the hair off his head for his role in the musical *The King and I* (1951) and he kept it shaved for the rest of his life, long before it became fashionable. The songs of George Gershwin, combined with the brilliant dancing of style icon Gene Kelly in *An American In Paris* (1951) or the veteran Fred Astaire as a womanizing playboy who meets his match in *The Belle Of New York* (1952) or *Silk Stockings* (1957) were all classics.

The wonderfully talented Jane Powell in lively musicals such as *Royal Wedding* (1951) in a classic duet with Fred Astaire singing (wait for it): 'How could you believe me when I said I loved you, when you know I've been a liar all my life.' She featured in a raft of films culminating in *Seven Brides for Seven Brothers* (1954) before going on to have a long successful career on stage. Anne Miller (dancer Lois Lane) in *Kiss me Kate* (1953) was claiming the world record for tap-dancing at 500 taps per minute. The big Hollywood musicals so favoured of MGM's dream factory eventually became passé and the last big musical *Gigi* was outdated even before it was released. The song of the decade (from the dull film of the same name) that has outsold all others, to the extent that it is still hot property today, is Bing Crosby's immortal *White Christmas* from 1954. Bing was one of the superstars of the 20th century. He appeared in nearly 100 films and recorded an incredible 1,850 records. His children's trusted Governess was Bridie Brennan from Borrisokane who accompanied Bing on his visit to the town in 1965 amid great excitement locally.

Cops 'N' Robbers

Crime has always been a key topic in film and the trend for the 50s began with John Huston's ***The Asphalt Jungle*** (1950) probably the first genuine heist movie. It was considered unique then in its honest portrayal of the professional preparation and execution of a crime.

For its time it was unusually detailed in recounting how the gangsters met and planned the robbery, leaving very little to chance. A young actress called Marilyn Monroe stars as the gangster's moll. It reflected gritty reality against the backdrop of the city streets portrayed as a jungle. It was not a box office success when first released for the reason that the criminals were considered much too sympathetically portrayed. But it was influential as a crafty exercise in character study and captured the imagination of film-makers elsewhere.

As a theme it was to be repeated many times with ***The Badlanders*** (1958) being a typical example. Many of the crime films were based on the novels of Raymond Chandler, who exclusively addressed the concerns of a male public. He was an extraordinary character with a mother from Waterford (where he spent some of his childhood) and a drink problem from which he eventually died in 1959. His most quoted line was that 'the streets were dark ... with something more than night'. When asked if he was concerned at what Hollywood was doing to his books he is alleged to have replied: 'They have done nothing to my books. Those are my books on the shelf. People who go to films are not going to read them anyway.'

Another recurring theme in crime films was the anti-hero, usually a veteran criminal who had put his past behind him, being lured back for the proverbial 'one last job'. Fatal. Fifty's crime provided raw material for many compelling courtroom dramas, the brilliant *Twelve Angry Men* (1957) and *Anatomy of a Murder* (1952) immediately springing to mind.

Stanley Kubrick, one of the most promising young film directors to have emerged in the 50s made a number of tense thrillers in *Killer's Kiss* (1955) and *The Killing* (1956) the latter which borrowed its theme from *The Asphalt Jungle*. Charles Laughton's nightmarish *The Night of the Hunter* (1955) has left behind the enduring image of Robert Mitchum – with his scary hooded eyes, something of a film noir icon – as a deranged preacher with the words 'love' and 'hate' tattooed on his fingers. *Touch of Evil* (1958) featured the bellicose Orson Welles as a corrupt policeman. Although the film is a routine B-movie, the cast assembled was like a 'who's who' of Hollywood's 'who-dunnits'. Alongside Welles was Charlton Heston, Janet Leigh, Marlene Dietrich, Mercedes McCambridge, Zsa Zsa Gabor and Joseph Cotton. Welles, a huge (in every sense of the word) exponent of classic Film Noir, had begun his acting career at the Gate Theatre in Dublin at age 16 under the tutelage of Michael MacLiammor and Hilton Edwards. He was to go on to have a distinguished career at all levels of the media but is particularly remembered for his role as Harry Lime in *The Third Man* (1949), where he made probably the most dramatic entrance in British cinema history as a man who's supposed to be dead. He never really conformed to Hollywood norms, preferring instead to infuse his films with a distinct European presence. Welles valued and nurtured all his Irish connections, including Dan O' Herlihy who went on to receive a Best Actor Academy Award nomination for the title role in *The Adventures of Robinson Crusoe* (1953). Actor Tyrone Power was also living in Dublin at this time. He was a third generation Irish-American actor, his grandfather (Tyrone Power also) was known throughout Ireland, England and America for his stage and music hall appearances. Tyrone Power was born in 1913 and starred in over 40 Hollywood films including *Mississippi Gambler* (1953), *Witness for the Prosecution* (1954) and *King of the Khyber Rifles* (1957) made shortly before his untimely death.

'You must remember this,
A kiss is just a kiss,
A sigh is just a sigh,
As time goes by'

An absolute giant of the 40s, Humphrey Bogart, made some very good films in the 50s including **The Caine Mutiny** and **The African Queen** in which he played opposite Katherine Hepburn in a kind of 'Beauty vs the Beast' format. Bogart was the only son of a wealthy New York surgeon and his acting was considered 'cutting edge' at that time. He had a lisp but rather than a handicap, he made good use of it and he had a particular way in which he could purse his lips into a sinister snarl. Always the loner, dressed in a hat and trench coat with the collar up, he was a foil for his arch enemies James Cagney or Sidney Greenstreet (The Fat Man). He usually played the hard boiled but likeable tough guy in detective movies. Bogie the Gumshoe was so urbane and cool as he sat in his seedy office in the half light, chain smoking as the sun tried to filter through closed venetian blinds. He was trying to figure out some beautiful but obviously desperate woman in a tight dress, with a past and a dim but dangerous boyfriend. This must be what was meant by the femme fatale. As soon as she had made her mysterious appearance and set the plot in some direction, a host of other characters would show up on cue. These would include the dutiful but dull lover, the bent cop and the psychotic gangster boss, almost all corrupted beyond redemption by the dark and cynical side of life. Lauren Bacall was only 19 years old when Howard Hawks cast her opposite Bogart in **To Have and Have Not** (1944) a wartime thriller based on a novel by Earnest Hemingway. They fell madly in love on set.

The interesting aspect of Film Noir from a Stella perspective, was the urban/rural divide. This is most evident in **On Dangerous Ground** (1951) where the city is portrayed as a jungle full of neurotic characters on the brink of ... well something sad or bad. For the hero in this film, salvation is found in the arms of a woman in a rural idyll as the mood softens. Postwar movies like **The Big Sleep** had already paved the way for this type of film which the French had already christened 'Film Noir'– the nocturnal world of dark shadows but Hollywood insiders rechristened it 'LA Noire'. Based on another story by novelist Raymond Chandler although the narrative is strong and eventful, the plot was a total mystery, beyond any comprehension. Not even Bogart or leading lady Lauren Bacall – for all the chemistry between them – seemed to have foggiest clue as to what was going on, never mind the audience. Yet this didn't seem to matter a great deal. It was well suited to a postwar audience who could relate to the low key lighting of rainy city streets, the vaguely defined mood of pessimism and undertones of paranoia. But dammit – it had atmosphere. In these movies wordplay mattered just as much as gunplay. Bogie could shoot from the lip as well as he could from the hip. Between clenched teeth he could render meaning and menace to such mundane lines as: 'Lets talk about the black bird.' It is some measure of his success that he is today quoted for lines he never actually used such as: 'Play it again, Sam' and 'Drop the gun, Looey.'

Bogart worked with the best including writers James Agee and Joe Mankiewicz who employed the classic flashback structure in *The Barefoot Contessa* (1954) by beginning with Ava Gardner's funeral and working back on her story. His last film was *The Harder They Fall* (1956). Humphrey Bogart died in 1957 aged 57 years, just weeks before the Stella opened its doors for the first time. He had ignored his doctors advice for treatment of throat cancer and continued to chain smoke and drink copious amounts of whiskey. Never having seemed stuck for a word on-screen, its easy to imagine what lines Bogie might have used if invited to the opening of the Stella. 'Louis (Paddy, Ned or Tim), I think this is the beginning of a beautiful friendship.'

Humphrey Bogart is ranked by the American Film Institute as the greatest actor in cinema history.

John Huston, the famous Hollywood director and Irish citizen – who lived in Galway – was closely connected with Bogart's film career. His first venture as a director was *The Maltese Falcon* starring the classic line up of Humphrey Bogart, Mary Astor, Peter Lorre and Sydney Greenstreet. Other great films of his were *Key Largo*, *The Treasure of Sierra Madre*, *The African Queen*, *The Red Badge of Courage* and *The Misfits.*

Occasionally in the 50s Hollywood excelled itself by producing a film – which though not belonging to any particular genre – was a thoughtful study of ordinary human relationships. An excellent example of this is the well crafted *The Bachelor Party* (1957) which takes on a typical New York office stag party overnight. As the night wears on and the alcohol kicks in, we observe the men's vulnerability and despair. An interesting period piece was *Seperate Tables* (1958), essentially a stage play set amongst the civilised boarders at an old fashioned English seaside hotel. A stellar 50s cast included David Niven, Deborah Kerr, Burt Lancaster, veteran Rita Hayworth and several British worthies such as Rod Taylor, Gladys Cooper and Wendy Hiller. A genteel drama which although could never set the pulse racing, nevertheless was professionally executed. Such a film also was *Marty* (1955) featuring the superb Ernest Borgine as a lovelorn butcher who fears he will never get a girl, and it deservedly won the Academy Award of that year. Or similarly but in a much lighter vein, there was *Harvey* (1950) a delightful comedy featuring James Stewart as a gormless drunk, whose sister wants to have certified insane. Relative insanity – great fun – they simply don't make them like that anymore!

None of the above would have made much of an impact on that annual Hollywood industrial circus known as the Academy Awards, or the Oscars. The history of Oscar winners and nominations is interesting as much for the outstanding films of the 1950's that were passed over, than the nominees and ultimate winners. Hard to comprehend now, that the following great films were not even nominated for Best Film; *Vertigo, North by Northwest, The Searchers*. But most surprisingly, an absolute classic *Some Like It Hot* was excluded in favour of *Ben-Hur* which received multiple awards, despite being not much better than the original silent epic of 1925.

STYLE & SUBSTANCE

The Eisenhower years (1953-1961) seemed to provide a line of boring conformist male actors who were good to look at but clones of one another almost. It's hard to distinguish the likes of Rock Hudson from a dozen lookalikes with high foreheads, big square jaws and oily hair. No wonder American cinema stagnated during this period. Thankfully there were some exceptions.

The sullen loner, James Dean became the Western world's first mixed up kid (teenager) in *East of Eden* and *Rebel without a Cause* made shortly before his sudden death. In the latter film Dean gives a superb performance as a frustrated teenager, rebelling against his weak father by means of alcohol, fighting and hot-rod car racing, usually partaking in all three at once. Born in 1931, as a young child, Dean was badly effected by the early death of his mother. She had a passion for poetry and gave him Byron as a second name. He joined drama school and his first break on television was given him by the legendary 'rosary priest' from Mayo, Fr Peyton. Given his background and outlook, it was not surprising that he would be portrayed as the embodiment of rebellious and alienated youth, full of grief and angst. Prior to his arrival in Hollywood, it was the generally accepted norm to expect young people to automatically obey their elders and behave themselves. If and when he did conform to expectations, it was with an air of rancour and reluctance. But he was perceived as a hero to young people standing up to those who thought they knew better.

In **Rebel without a Cause** one of the gang of juveniles is played by the enigmatic actor and photographer Denis Hopper, then just 18 years of age. The two were good friends and both played together once again alongside Elizabeth Taylor and Rock Hudson in the long drawn out epic *Giant*. Trying to come to terms with manhood seemed to drive him crazy. With the collaboration of the enigmatic film director, Nicholas Ray, they virtually invented and branded the 1950's juvenile delinquent genre. It was said that Dean was playing himself, a surly rebel who would not conform. Constantly agonising: 'What do you do when you have to be a man?' Yet he seemed to hit a nerve in the American psyche. He influenced teenagers all over the world, presenting them with an image totally distinct from that of their parents. Fame was to become eternal when (shortly after being booked for speeding) he crashed his silver Porsche

Spyder at over 90 mph. He died aged 24 years, having just completed his final film *Giant*. Ironically he was driving to Salinas in California, the birthplace and final resting place of novelist John Steinbeck, the author of *East of Eden*. The tragic novel is itself set in Salinas in 1917, which Steinbeck believed typified small town America of the time. It is in effect the Biblical story of Cain and Able put in a contemporary setting. The release of *Giant* after Dean's death ensured that never before had anyone achieved such lasting fame on just three films in an 18 month career. Just like Marilyn Monroe, he is today regarded as a fashion icon of American pop culture of the 1950's.

Another James, James Bond – Secret Agent 007 – made his appearance in the Stella in *Dr No*, the very first Bond film. Technically it wasn't the actor's first appearance there, as he had already featured in *Darby O'Gill and the Little People* (1959) as a 'Dublin Man'. He even sang a 'come-all-ye' entitled 'Pretty Irish Girl', giving no hint of what his cinematic future held in store. We kids wondered if he was related to the Bonds of Uskane, but someone mentioned the actor's name was Sean Connery, so we reckoned he was more likely to be from Roscrea. Then, when we heard that accent ('shaken not stirred') we knew he must be from Russia or somewhere, we had never heard anyone speak like that in the films before. With the sudden appearance of bikini clad Ursuala Andress still dripping wet from a blue sea, the focus shifted quickly away from Bond's unimportant identity.

Whether you love him for his brooding intensity or hate him for mumbling his lines, Marlon Brando carved his own special niche in film over many decades. He was an early adherent to the Stravinski or method style. Nowhere was this better exemplified than in *On the Waterfront* (1954) which won eight Oscars including Best Actor for Brando. Based on a true story around Hoboken Docks, New Jersey, the code on the waterfront was D&D – Deaf and Dumb. Nobody spoke to the authorities and the mob ruled. Considered a classic of American realistic drama and with a great performance from Rod Steiger. The immortal lines from the end of this film are well loved; 'Charlie, oh Charlie. You don't understand, I could have had class. I could have been a contender!'

Brando never became an icon to the same levels as James Dean or Marilyn Monroe for the simple reason that he grew old in public, virtually on screen. In his first film *The Men* (1950) Brando plays a young solider paralysed from the waist down. To get himself totally into the role, he spent a month in an army hospital in a wheelchair – that's method apparently. In *The Wild One* (1953) Brando plays a black leather clad leader of a motorcycle gang playing opposite Mary Murphy – the sheriff's daughter – who asked Brando what he was rebelling against, 'What've you got?' he replied.

One of the most famous and successful directors of all time was the supreme master of suspense Alfred Hitchcock born in 1900, who averaged a film a year over a 50 year career. He was a genius and his name became synonymous with thrillers as he continued to manipulate audiences with such classics such as *North by Northwest, Strangers On a Train, The Trouble with Harry, To Catch a Thief, Rear Window, The Wrong Man, The Man Who Knew Too Much,* and *Dial M For Murder*.

Vertigo (1958) was such a significant film that it led to confusion about the medical term in the title. It was confused with acrophobia – a fear of heights – whereas vertigo is quite distinct and is characterized by a feeling of movement when standing, most common among women over 50.

Every odd detail in a Hitchcock film is there for a reason and mistaken identity was a theme he used to the full. He was the doyen of auto-suggestion and the sublime fear of the unseen in film. His goal was suspense not horror and he achieved this by giving the viewer information not known to the main characters. In addition to film, he also branched out to television and his familiar dark profile became universally known on the cover of books and magazines. Although the 50s were his most productive period, he could be said to have had four different careers in film over his lifetime.

Firstly in silent movies – which he regarded as the purest form of cinema and he never abandoned its principles – then in sound (both of these in England) to be followed by Hollywood in the 40s and finally colour from 1952. Arguably his best period began with ***Rear Window*** in 1954 and ended with ***Psycho*** in 1960. Add to that a further career in television which began with ***Alfred Hitchcock Presents*** in 1955, the same year he became a US citizen. The show was always introduced by Hitchcock in ponderous tones 'Good evening ... My name is Alfred Hitchcock.' An indelible image from our 1960s childhood in Borrisokane is that of Hitchcock's iconic silhouette centre screen on black and white television, to the familiar theme music of ***Funeral march of a Marionette***. The show ran for seven years. There was at that time a false rumour around that Hitchcock had actually been born in Borrisokane. This arose because of the other Hitchcock connection, his namesake Reginald Hitchcock (Rex Ingram) who had lived in the Rectory. NB: I hope you are paying attention reader, because this bit can be very confusing. There were many similarities between the pair but for the record, Alfred Hitchcock was born in the East End of London in 1899. He was educated by the Jesuits at St Ignatius College, London and his only known Irish connections were distant Irish relatives, living in Liverpool, on his mother's side of the family by the name of Whelan.

In another coincidence between the two men Alfred Hitchcock's sister Nellie married an Irishman called Ingram. Rex Ingram did meet up with Alfred Hitchcock when the younger Englishman first came over to Hollywood. Rex Ingram's advice was to drop the name of Hitchcock altogether as 'you will not get very far in Hollywood with a name like that.' Alfred Hitchcock was the definitive Englishman in Hollywood.

He described film as being just the same as life 'with the boring bits taken out'. He could be said to have some Borrisokane characteristics for sure. He had a marvelously impish sense of humour. With his expressionless face, never smiling and deadly serious tone of voice, he once caused total consternation on a crowded lift by muttering audibly to a companion, 'I never thought the old man would bleed so much.'

In an interview, when asked for his advice on how long a suspense film should be, his reply was; 'The length of any film should be directly related to the endurance of the human bladder.'

Hitchcock's films were not particularly noted for dialogue, he used the camera to tell the story much in the best traditions of silent cinema. He usually played a small cameo role in his films but it had to be early on, so as not to distract the audience from the plot while they were watching out for him.

He had a penchant for having blonde women in his lead roles and it was Hitchcock who discovered one of the great film stars of the time, the elegant and beautiful Grace Kelly. An American of Irish extraction, she first came to prominence in **High Noon** (1952) as the peace loving wife of Sheriff Gary Cooper. Interestingly, she was always cast opposite much older men which was to resonate in later life and marriage. In *Mogambo* (1953) she played opposite Clark Gable and Ava Gardner who acted her off the stage. Her first appearance in a Hitchcock movie was *Dial M for Murder* (1954) but it was her classy role in Hitchcock's *Rear Window* (1954) that set her apart as a star. Monaco was the colourful location of her next alliance with Hitchcock when playing opposite the suave Cary Grant, she starred in *To Catch a Thief* (1955). She was subsequently dubbed the 'Ice-Maiden' but she swapped her film career for that of real life princess when she married the more senior Prince Albert of Monaco in 1955. Her last film was *The Swan* (1956) alongside Alec Guinness, in which she played the designer role of a princess who is required to put duty before love. Hitchcock tried to lure her back but she declined the role in *Marine* (1964) and there was to be no comeback for the princess with the enchanting screen presence. Both love and duty came first it would seem and she died tragically in a car crash. Considered an indifferent actor but an absolutely enchanting screen presence she is remembered lovingly in many ways, not least as the reason why so many American girls are given the Christian name of Kelly (Kelley). She is ranked as 13th greatest female star ever by the American Film Institute.

War Movies

War films were most definitely not a true portrayal of the many world conflicts of a violent 20th Century. They were interesting if a bit predictable, some of them having been shot for propaganda purposes. The title was often the most exciting aspect with the description 'Hell' being used, or overused, in the title of many films.

Most of them were as wooden as *The Wooden Horse* (1950) or as damp as *The Frogmen* (1951) or *The Gift Horse* (1952) which 'also ran'. The kids would have been familiar with this genre from their readership of British comics such as the Victor or the Hotspur, which traded daily in an active second hand swap market. The British army chaps were quickly recognisable. Jolly chipper types, great smokers with a devilish sense of humour. They could rightly be described as dapper, although their use of the English language was odd. For example, they would say things like 'piece of cake' when the situation clearly had nothing to do with confectionery. But they could outwit the Germans any day. In *The Colditz Story* (1955) the prison was supposed to be a top security jail for the incarceration of high-ranking British officers. Perhaps the first flaw was the odd German logic of putting all of the top escapees together in the same prison. Ironically, life in Colditz was a bit of a doddle by comparison with action on the front line. The well fed inmates (including John Mills and Ian Carmichael) had plenty of food, cigarettes, chewing gum and all they could ask for down to drag pantomime. But for reasons obvious only to themselves, the British aristo types wanted to do the honourable thing and break out, to finish off the war on a high note, perhaps. For all its hype and exciting background music this was one limp movie. Perhaps it should have been renamed the 'Butlinz' story.

Similarly, *From Here to Eternity* (1953) although set amongst US army officers in Hawaii during Pearl Harbour, is probably more about sexual relations than war. However, the sizzling scene featuring Burt Lancaster and Deborah Kerr's passionate embrace whilst tumbling around the incoming tide would certainly have caused its own conflict and raised temperatures in the morally uptight Ireland of 1953.

One of the lesser drawbacks of being on the losing side in a world conflict is the creation of the racist stereotype enemy. Take the German soldiers as portrayed in British and American 'war' films. There were two fairly distinct types. Firstly, the lower ranking ones were sullen thick necked fellas usually bald with a tendency to facial contortions. They existed only to take orders. Their officers were more aristocratic looking with steely grey eyes, blond hair carefully slicked back, high cheekbones (scar optional) and whose favourite line which they spoke from a corner of their mouth usually began: 'When ve vin der var ...' or alternatively 'For you the var is over.'

These stereotypes clearly influenced the young audiences at the time. In Bray district court, a German national was brought on front of a district court judge on a charge of larceny in the town. The defendant indicated that he could speak no English and the judge appealed to the gallery for anyone who could help. A lanky youth (up on some minor charge) immediately offered his services and begun to interrogate the defendant. 'Vas iss your naam?' He even got as far as 'Ve haf vaws of making you talk' before being speedily ejected from the bemused courtroom.

The Yankee soldiers were much more varied and nearly all had crew-cuts and medallions. But don't the mention the Japanese. They seemed to live up coconut trees and had the worst lines usually something like 'Baanzaiiiaaaaaagh' as some GI blew yet another cowardly sniper out of his perch. The odd Irishman turned up, usually stone mad and could be depended upon to get blown up early on.

The most successful war film of the 1950s was the

Bridge over the River Kwai. It was set in a Japanese POW camp where prisoners are forced to work on building a railway line between Singapore and India. The film is another portrayal of the pure futility of war as represented by a bridge which the prisoners try to construct and destroy at the same time. The superb acting of Alec Guinness and William Hawkings ensured that the film literally ran away with the 1957 Academy Awards and an Oscar for Sir Alec Guinness despite its confused ending. Again, it does not accurately depict the true horror of the deaths of 16,000 allied POWs.

Norman Mailer's best-selling war novel *The Naked and the Dead* in 1948 was a huge influence on the American war films of the 50s. Another good example was *The Red Badge of Courage* (1951) with Audie Murphy (America's most decorated war hero in World War 2) playing the lead role. It focused on war without the usual hype or glory as experienced by a scared young soldier. Here the lead was portrayed as an ordinary human being in uniform, caught up in the awful horrors of war. Unfortunately, the studios went on to exploit Murphy's own glory in some truly cringe inducing pictures like *To Hell And Back* (1955). Another notable war film of the period shot in authentic castles was the excellent *Paths of Glory* (1957) which explored corruption in the French Army. The story goes that the producers wanted a typically happy ending. The director Stanley Kubrick quite rightly pointed out that it was a war film, a genre which was a bit short on happy endings and besides he was sticking to the original story-line. But they were persistent. Before making the final cut he allegedly received an important phone call; 'Got your happy ending, Stanley ... we will let the Germans win and the three French lads can go home.'

War at sea appeared a more leisurely affair if *Mr Roberts* (1955) was anything to go by. The star studded cast including Henry Fonda in the title role as the stoical supply officer, James Cagney – the villainous captain and superb Jack Lemmon is the young ensign. The plot concerns the conflicts between the various crew members as much as it does the war. The climax of the film comes when Fonda, in a minute bit of cinema history, throws the ship's rubber plant overboard – hardly Armageddon. The film was the culmination of the play of the same name which had enjoyed 1000 stage productions on Broadway where it proved a strong vehicle for Fonda's versatile acting talents. It brought together again the team of John Ford and Henry Fonda and there were many battles between these two during shooting.

Again, the war conveniently melted into the background to allow drunken marine (Robert Mitchum) to charm an Irish nun (Deborah Kerr) in *Heaven Knows Mr Allison* (1957). Burt Lancaster had the attentions of *South Sea Woman* (1953) to take his mind off war in the Pacific while he and Clarke Gable were getting fierce cranky with each other in the confines of the submarine in *Run Silent, Run Deep* (1958). But at the salty bottom of this nautical non sequitur, the nadir of filmic ship wrecks has to be *Sea Wife* (1957) featuring Captain Richard Burton and Joan Collins as –

yes, another! – nun. A young Stella audience sat longing for a U-Boat or Air attack to put an end to it. ***D-Day – the Sixth of June*** (1956) was a meek attempt at the invasion of Normandy.

The Longest Day came to the Stella in the 60s, playing for three nights to full houses. It was based on the book of the same name by Dubliner Corneilus Ryan who had covered the actual event as war correspondent for the Daily Telegraph. Many of the extras on the Normandy beaches were ex-infantrymen who had fought and survived the invasion there 18 years earlier. Apparently it was exactly as it had been in 1944. Shot in black and white and plenty of grey it was certainly the longest film ever shown there, running for over three hours. Everybody who was anybody in film turned up in the cast, with 'The Dook' himself, John Wayne, smoking a big cigar as he swapped his horse for a jeep. Unlike most of the extras taking part, Wayne the archetypical American hero had been unavailable during the real thing and had never fought in World War II. But this film had everything any schoolchild could ask for. Based on historical fact, it showed how individuals dealt with their surroundings amid expectation and fear but like all good stories it was made up of fragments, a bit of this and a bit of that. We had cameos of guys waiting for action for ages on old ships, hard bitten young Yanks writing home to Mum as frame by frame we met the players.

So there was background, build-up and the action when it came gave us some truly memorable individual moments. For example, the paratroopers zeroing in on

France with some landing lightly, some not so good, hanging out of church steeples as air-raid sirens blared and manic SS blazed away with their machine-guns. One poor unfortunate landed through the glass roof of a Nazi occupied greenhouse. A truly great moments in the film features a German 'look-out' (with dialogue suitably subtitled) in a pillbox on the coast of France. He routinely scans the horizon with his binoculars, and as usual there is nothing to see, just a bit of fog on the channel. Before changing shift moments later he looks again. Ho-Hum. This time through his binoculars he sees the biggest armada of ships ever assembled on planet earth heading straight for him! The ultimate moment, greeted with a mixture of shock, incredulity, and pandemonium!

HORROR OF HORRORS

Horror was all the rage with plenty of blood and gore from the living, the dead and the half alive/dead. The heyday of horror was the 1930s but many of these films were still in vogue in the 50s. In America, a youthful Roger Corman drew on the creations of Edgar Allan Poe to good effect, while in England, Hammer Films specialised in the horror genre with Boris Karloff being the leading light (dark?). They were now playing to gullible audiences whose own dark folk memories were filled with ghosts, fairies and banshees. People got really caught up in the horror films, feeling the same terror as the characters but enjoying it all from the relative safety of their seats.

The themes were usually the unknown, demons or the dead. There were horror films ranging from the good to the bad to the downright hilarious. Scariest moment just had to be in the opening scenes of *The*

Black Sleep (1956). Bit player, Tor Johnson, a bald heavy set ex-wrestler, played the part of a failed human cloning experiment. When first seen in the film, his head is bowed revealing just his polished dome. As he raises his scowling face to look at his audience, only the stark whites of his eyes are visible – he has no pupils! The truly eerie ambience of nightmares.

Good old nut-necked Boris Karloff became familiar and eminently likeable in *Frankenstein*. Not so pleasant was the good doctor's creation as portrayed in Peter Cushing's Hammer version of *The Revenge of Frankenstein* (1958). But it was Dracula who received top billing especially with the suitably sinister Christopher Lee as the star in films like *Blood of Dracula* or *Horror of Dracula*. In *Dracula* (1958) we first see the Count in shadow but stepping into the light to politely introduce himself. We are momentarily lulled before the shock of his next appearance. The dark master of understatement: 'I never drink ... wine.'

We were later to learn that the author of Dracula was Dubliner Bram Stoker. He was feeble as a youth, being bedridden until the age of twelve. His mother tended him daily and she told him many stories of her own first hand experience of the Famine in her native Roscommon. She had seen dreadful things like people drinking the blood of live cattle and bodies being literally pushed into coffins. In these horrendous circumstances it would have been all to easy to believe that the restless dead stalked the land nightly. He was fascinated to learn of the blood feeding bats of South America. All of this was to inspire Stoker in his literary themes and it is believed that his original concept of the vampire figure was an analogy for the hated landlord, sucking the life blood from the common people. He linked this with the story of 'Vlad the Impaler' in the Baltics and so Count Dracula, the legendary character most often portrayed in horror films was born. On horror nights in the Stella, the foyer could get quite crowded during the scary bits with many of the locals preferring to linger on there for a smoke and a chat in absolutely no hurry back to the show. Inside some of the harder cases were relishing every moment. There were two old ladies who absolutely lived for the horror films and fear was not a factor. The eerie graveyard silence in *A Bucket of Blood* (1959) was broken once with the immortal lines from the back of the house ... 'Jays Marge, will ya look at the head of that fella ... and the price of turnips.'

Then there was the film *The 5000 Fingers of Dr T* (1953), a great title and a real curiosity but a bizarre piece of surrealism that defied genre. The basic premise of many of these films was so patently incredible that it was simply, well, unbelievable. In *The Fly* (1958) we are asked to believe that the scientist has been given the head of a fly. The unfortunate was part-man and part blue bottle. Even ould Pakie, who believed that the world was flat wasn't having any of this. However, he wasn't so nonplussed with *Them* (1954) with its theme of mutation, enough to frighten the daylights out of anyone. *In Eyes without a Face* (1959) the very concept of the mad scientist and his assistant attempting to rebuild the face of a mutilated girl was more convincing.

The scariest films shown at the Stella were thought to be *The Mummy* series, produced by Hammer Films at their Bray Studios. The heavily bandaged one had been central to horror movies since the 1920s but was successfully revived by Hammer Films in 1959 with Christopher Lee in the lead role. For some reason, young and old veterans of Dracula, Frankenstein, or Fu Manchu would run from their seats at the first sight of the Mummy's gnarled hands and unseeing eyes in films like *The Mummy's Tomb*.

Cycling home alone at midnight down the dark lane past the workhouse graveyard with its mass of unmarked famine graves and overhanging trees could be an unnerving experience after one of these films. For good measure, many of the film directors held on to their own peculiar sense of humour when making horror films and even put the odd joke over on the audience for their own amusement. In *The Black Cat*, Boris Karloff played the part of a devil worshipper. Standing on a plinth in robes, with a torch raised in his right hand he begun chanting the words 'Cave Canem' over and over to which the assembled heathens responded 'Cum Grano Salis'. Hairy stuff right enough, until we realise that Cave Canum is the Latin for 'Beware of the Dog' and Cum Grano Salus translates to 'With a grain of salt'.

SCIENCE FICTION

The paranoia of the Cold War period was immediately reflected in the spate of science fiction films in this era of satellites and the Sputnik. Usually the earth was in grave danger from moving blobs (of strawberry jam), mutant lizards, lobster-like parasites, invading pods or giant flesh eating spiders in imaginative films with marvellous titles such as ***When Worlds Collide*** (1951), ***The Thing From Another World*** (1951), ***Invaders from Mars*** (1953), ***The War of The Worlds*** (1953), ***Devil Girl from Mars*** (1954), ***Them*** (1954), ***The Quartermass Experiment*** (1955), ***Invasion Of The Body Snatchers*** (1956), ***Invasion of the Saucer Men*** (1957), ***It Conquered the World*** (1956), ***The Brain from Planet Arous*** (1957), ***Not of this Earth*** (1957), ***Attack of the Crab Monsters*** (1957), and ***The Tingler*** (1959). The mass appeal of these films was greatly enhanced by the dramatic images of legendary film poster artist Reynold Brown. His luridly colourful and engaging posters for films such as ***Creature from the***

Lagoon (1957) with its unlikely monolith monster, elevated the whole genre to a new level. The work of brilliant animator Ray Harryhausen was monumental in this genre. A youthful Leslie Neilson cut his proverbial acting teeth in *Forbidden Planet* (1956) alongside Robby the Robot. Mind you, the more one observed of irrational human behaviour on the screen, the stronger the case became for direct rule from Mars. In *The Day The Earth Stood Still* (1951) a peaceful alien along with his giant robot minder commute to Washington via flying saucer to warn mankind to give up war or face retribution. Fair enough. Now why the Americans as portrayed in the film could make no serious effort to properly communicate with this harmless looking pair is very hard to understand. Was it because they were different. In this case the robot's name was Gort so surely being called after the friendliest town in the west of Ireland would have given the Yanks some ground for empathy. But no, American style hysteria was always going to win the day, giving rise to the first great traffic jams on our planet – total gridlock! Little wonder those Martians went home taking a mental note to erase destination earth from their holiday itinerary next year. And the dialogue in these films was never prone to understatement.

In the opening scenes from *It Came From Outer Space* (1953) as the male and female lead settle in to domestic bliss on their ranch, a fiery object shoots across the night sky, crashing to earth nearby. 'Its like nothing we've seen before ... this may be the biggest thing that's ever happened!' Unfortunately after the initial excitement of the landing, it was hard to sustain the suspense in these films. Amongst other contenders for worst films of all time was Ed Wood's *Plan 9 from Outer Space* (1958). It included veteran creepies Tor Johnson and Bela Lugosi, the latter managing to die during the early stages of filming yet he makes it to the credits at the end. *Earth Versus The Flying Saucer* (1956) is a similar cosmic damp squib with its pathetic destruction of Lego block buildings.

'Not on such a nice afternoon was the capital going to be destroyed,' the voice-over told us, as the aliens made their move. A woman drops her handbag in the panic, hesitates and leaves it after her. It looked that grim before Earth finally won by a short head. And we learned that 'clones' meant more than a town in Monaghan and speaking of Monaghan, in 1953, it did it's fair share for the U.F.O Industry, when Desmond Leslie (of Castle Leslie) co-wrote the very sucessful book *Flying Saucers have Landed* which became a handbook for 'Space Cadets' everywhere.

In the naff and tawdry realm of 1950's science fiction films, the arena is full of contenders jostling for position in a race to the bottom for the uncoveted title of 'worst film ever made'. Despite the fact that none of the above would be rated by Mr Halliwell in his guide, there is something innocent and lovable about these films. Take *20 Million Miles from Earth* which ticks all the boxes in the diminishing nebula of cosmic dross. Although shot in gorgeous – if garish – colour, in Sicily and Italy, the plot concerning a scaly monster from Venus evading capture, is glacial in movement and the acting is pure ham. That said, as period curiosity pieces these films can be very relaxing to watch, particularly if the viewer is lulled and aided by a mind and mood altering substance like a pint of stout, maybe. It's almost guaranteed to get you in the 'space', if that's what you're after! This dialogue tells all, 'One thing's for sure. Inspector Clay is dead, murdered and somebody's responsible!'

However, what cinemagoer of the period could possibly resist films with such titles as **Destination Moon** (1950), **The Beast from 20,000 Fathoms** (1953), **This Island Earth** (1955), **It Came from Beneath the Sea** (1955), **The She Creature** (1956), **Twenty Million Miles to Earth** (1957), **The Incredible Shrinking Man** (1957), **Not of this Earth** (1957), **From the Earth to the Moon** (1958), **War of the Colossal Beast** (1958), or **Attack of the Fifty Foot Woman** (1958). In the Stella, initial audience suspense and even incredulity gave way to cynicism and humour. In an early scene from **The Thing** we meet the hero and his companion under grave threat from a malevolent life force from outer space. The tension becomes palpable as the companions become separated in a steamy marsh. With panic rising the hero cries out through the darkening gloom:

'Where are you ... Where are you?'

From the back of the cinema hall comes the helpful response, 'I'm above beyont in the balcony'

FILM UK

Despite the strong outpouring of talent, mainly from the Royal Academy of Dramatic Arts but also from Joan Littlewood's theatre workshop, the proud traditions of the British film industry were not so evident in the 1950's. During the coming decade, it was not destined to scale the heights of broad appeal achieved in the 40s, when over 40 films a year were released from Pinewood, Elstree and Shepperton Studios. This had been the era of wartime classics such as ***Great Expectations, The Red Shoes, Oliver Twist, Black Narcissus, Brighton Rock, Hamlet, Brief Encounter, The Life and Times of Col. Blimp, Henry V., Mrs Miniver, Whiskey Galore*** ('Ay, giz a dram of haig dimple') but especially the brilliantly surreal and futuristic ***A Matter of Life and Death***. Have you seen this one? We're just minutes into the film and David Niven is sitting there in his burning bomber about to crash land and meet his death. Finally he gets through on his radio to base camp. A lovely concerned American girl answers the phone. So what are they going to chat about in his last 60 seconds or is there time for romance?

British cinema came close to producing its own Film Noir with films such as *The Big Clock, Night and the City* and *Brighton Rock* set in a little England of drab tea rooms and smoky Victorian pubs. The end of the decade had rendered the best British film of them all, Carol Reed's *The Third Man*. This film was a huge success in Ireland and Anton Karas came to Dublin to play to packed houses on his zither, receiving encores for the 'Harry Lime' theme. By the 50s, the industry was in something of a slump with American domination being a growing factor as the best of British talent was wooed to Hollywood. The Boulting brothers, John and Roy, consistently produced the finest comedy and satire with films like *The Magic Box* (1951), *Private's Progress* (1956) and *I'm All Right Jack* (1956). John Mills was a huge influence as director and actor kicking off the decade with black humour in *Mr Denning Drives North* (1951).

The biggest British box office draw of the time was Dirk Bogarde with such early successes as *The Blue Lamp* (1950), *Appointment in London* (1953), *For Better or Worse* (1954), *Doctor in The House* (1954), and *Doctor at Sea* (1955). Bogarde was considered a very fine actor who went on to play darker and more complex roles in the following decades. The inimitable veteran Charles Laughton played his best role of the decade in *Hobson's Choice* (1954). In *The Captains Paradise* (1953) he played the part of a ferry boat captain with a wife in each port.

The poor state of the industry was underlined by the

sale of the world famous Ealing studios in London to
the BBC in 1956. Ealing Studios had produced a series
of classic films in the best traditions of subtle British
comedy, known as 'The Ealing Comedies'. These films
were a whimsical portrait of a postwar genteel England
of little old landladies offering cups of tea, likeable
rogues or 'spivs' and shiny red buses in the rain. The
most notable of these being **Passport to Pimlico**
(1950), **The Lavender Hill Mob** (1951), **The Man in
the White Suit** (1951), and **The Lady-killers** (1955)
the latter featuring a cherubic Peter Sellers as a violin
player. In the main these films were built around the
extraordinary versatile acting talents of one man – Alec
Guinness. Following rave reviews, he was embarrassed
at the media description of 'Star' and he made it clear
that his job was that of an Actor.

In **Kind Hearts and Coronets** (1950) Guinness
played all eight (both male and female) members of an
aristocratic family who were to be eliminated by Denis
Price to enable him to get his hands on the family
jewels. **The Smallest Show on Earth** (1957) was itself
a farewell tribute to old style cinema. The plot line
consists of a young couple who inherit an old flea pit of
a cinema and try to make it pay. It features Peter Sellers
as the drunken projectionist. Although a reasonably
watchable film, how it beat **High Noon** that year to
claim an Oscar will forever remain a mystery.

A brilliant script underpinned the comedy **Genevieve**
(1953) a film set at the London to Brighton car rally.
Despite the understandably postwar upbeat feel to the

films early in the decade, the industry latterly seemed to lose confidence and concentrate on comedy of the crude and rude variety and the first of the 'Carry On' series, **Carry on Sergeant** was shot in 1958.

Colombia/Yeoman were content to pour out dross like **Sword of Sherwood Forest** with the aptly named Richard Green prancing around the woods clad in green tights. One of the most popular stars at this time was Norman Wisdom whose style of comedy made him a big favourite with the Stella audiences. In fairness there were notable war films such as **The Cruel Sea, The Desert Rats**, and **Ice Cold in Alex**. British detective films were extremely drab in comparison to their American counterparts. The overworked police inspector **Gideon of Scotland Yard** (1959) bumbling around looking for clues was wholly uninspiring.

Roy Ward Baker's Titanic melodrama **A Night to Remember** filmed in a swimming pool in Ruislip, London, was released in 1958. It has aged well and given the highly predictable ending, is as good as any film made about the ill fated ship. Kenneth More's last spoken lines in the film may be unintentionally metaphoric in reflecting disillusionment and lack of confidence in the industry at that time: 'I don't think I shall ever feel sure again ... about anything. '

It wasn't until the very end of the 1950s that British films began to question traditional certainties and reflect social issues and the output did have an impact on society. This trend began with **Tiger Bay** (1957), **Room at the Top** (1958), **Look Back in Anger** (1959), and ***A Taste of Honey*** (1960) which revealed whole new possibilities of gritty urban realism. The relationships between men and women were examined in detail against the industrial backdrop of the day. However from the Borris audience's perspective these did not amount to much. Gritty urban realism with a heavy social message is all very well in its place and time, but not in the Stella where people came to the pictures to escape gritty rural reality.

WORLD CINEMA

'All the world's a stage ...'
– William Shakespeare

The 1950s witnessed hugely exciting influences and developments in cinema internationally which bypassed Ireland completely. Distinctive national genres began to flourish which entertained, educated and informed like never before. Therefore the Americans cornered the musicals, the Germans went nostalgic with their 'Heimat' films, the French captured romantic cinema and the Swedes did depression like nobody else. Anglo American films had always been popular in countries like France, Spain and Italy (in particular) where they were 'dubbed' into the appropriate language to suit local audiences. Apparently, after World War Two, one of the concessions demanded by the US was that American films be given free access to French cinemas. And what about the French, the people who had after all invented cinema (even the word is French) in 1895 in that petit town by the Mer-La Ciotat with les freres Lumiere toiling away in the Eden cinema. But that was silent cinema they created, a truly universal product that could be seen and appreciated anywhere in the world. For many purists, the birth of the 'talkies' represented the death of early cinema in its purist form and narrowed its focus to those countries where the dialogue was understood without the need for subtitles. In general, there were young directors emerging through the postwar era of reconstruction. France's Henri-George Clouzot gave us one of the greatest films of the 50s – **The Wages of Fear** (**Le Salaire De La Peur)** (1953). It involves four desperate men who sign up for a suicide mission to transport trucks full of nitroglycerine to blow up a burning oil field. The suspense and sense of impending doom in the film is held throughout, with the characters themselves divided between preventive action (one character in particular) and controlled panic (the other three) grip the audience from start to finish. France also provided one of the funniest films of the decade with **Monsieur Hulot's Holiday** (1953). As well as Francois Truffaut's autobiographical debut **Les Quatre Cent Coups** (1959).

The phrase 'nouvelle vague' was coined in France in 1957 and this heralded in the 'new wave.' The trust of this movement gave rise to shooting films much more quickly and cheaply than the established directors.

France was credited with leading the field but once started, the flow of ideas, films and stars across differing cultures soon left Hollywood in the shade. Throughout the following years, its influence spread to the English speaking film world.

Many country's film industry seemed dominated by individual giants such Spain's Louis Bunuel, Poland's Andrzej Wajda and Sweden's Ingmar Bergman who made the dinfinitive statement on cinema when he said, 'Film as dream, film as music. No art passes our conscience in the way film does, and goes directly to our feelings, deep down into the dark rooms of our souls.' Bergman had effectively 'defected' from Hollywood's crass commercialism to direct *The Seventh Seal* (1957). With its unique premise of Death vs a Knight in a deadly game of chess, the image of Max Von Sydow as the wandering knight remains a most durable image in world cinema. He had no time for the 'weasel wording' of the American industry and he summed up his philosophy with stunning simplicity, 'What matters most in life,' he stated, 'is being able to contact another human being.' This honest approach would not have impressed the money mad moguls of Hollywood. This outlook was shared by Italy's Fellini whose theme was the search for meaning and purpose in life in films like *La Strada* (1954). Italy showed that it had more to offer than a staple diet of 'Spaghetti Westerns'. Italian neo-realists began shooting stories on the street where they happened.

In India, the great humanist film maker Satyajit Ray

ruled supreme. His first film ***Panther Panchali*** (1955) was probably one of the finest directorial debuts ever, capturing as it did the sheer intensity of childhood. His ***World of Apu*** (1958) was the second of a classic trilogy portraying the story of Apu, a young boy growing up in poverty in rural India with background music by Ravi Shankar. Japan, in contrast to Western cinema enjoyed huge growth at this time. Again just one individual seemed to dominate, Akira Kurosawa whose reflection of the primitive world of ***Seven Samurai*** (1954) is acknowledged as one of the great action classics of world cinema. This visually stunning film was hugely influential and if the ultimate accolade of a film is the remake, then this film was remade by John Sturges in the following decade as ***The Magnificent Seven,*** while Japan's Yojimbo also formed the basis for ***A Fistful of Dollars***. But all of this was in the clouds, light years away and well over the heads of the Stella kids.

FILM IN IRELAND

The history of Irish film in the 50s or any other era is a strange and delicate hybrid. It is noteworthy that the Cork International Film Festival began in 1953 and has achieved enduring influence and success for almost 60 years. The Irish film industry had always been something of a misnomer as there had never been a meaningful native film industry here, despite brave individual efforts. These could be exemplified by the making of the 1930s film *The Dawn*, cobbled together through the goodwill of the people of Killarney under the inspired leadership of enterprising garage owner Tom Cooper.

During the shooting of this film, electricity consumption for Killarney increased tenfold. Cooper had cleverly anticipated this and he had appointed the General Manager of the ESB on to the board of directors. It was debatable as to what constituted an 'Irish' film, as the ones made in Ireland then were financed by capital from abroad, usually British or American money. For example, *Henry V* (featuring Laurence Oliver) was shot in Powerscourt, Enniskerry, Co. Wicklow during World War 2 as an almost totally British production. Oliver brought together 200 riders and 500 foot soldiers from the Local Defence Force (LDF) to re-enact the battle of Agincourt. During the 50s, the industry was dependent on American producers and towards the end of the decade, the overflow from the British film industry. There were a number of Irish-themed films made in the UK but too many of these were 'stage Irish' or 'Oirish'. Belfast born writer Brian Desmond Hurst directed the best version of *Scrooge* (1951) with the brilliant Alastair Sim playing the lead role. But there were many duds including; *Jack of All Maids* (1951) featuring the legendary Abbey actor Jack MacGowran who also starred alongside Niall MacGinnis and Eileen Herlie in *She Didn't Say No* (1958), the story of a young Irish widow with five illegitimate children each by a different father. *The March Hare* (1956) starring Peggy Cummins and Terence Morgan was in similar vein. *A Tale of Five Cities* shot in London in 1951 with Gina Lollobrigida has a cameo of Irish interest in that it features Andy Irvine as a boy. This was before the well loved musician came to Ireland and formed a key part of Planxty and other great traditional and folk groups. Another musical connection is Leo Rowsome who plays the Uilleann Pipes in *Broth Of A Boy* (1959) which featured Barry Fitzgerald in his last film, playing the oldest man in the world.

Without doubt, the most influential 'Irish' film of the decade was *The Quiet Man* a virtual 'tour-de-force' spectacle of Irish cinema. The story began in 1933, when an American newspaper published a short story by Maurice Walsh called 'Green Rushes' as part of a trilogy of short stories known as *Three Roads*. Dripping with sentimentality, it attracted the attentions of Hollywood producer John Ford – not noted for his largesse – who promptly paid $10 for the film rights. He toted it around various studios until Republic Studio Productions reluctantly agreed to take it on based on Ford's track record. The cast and crew descended on the tiny village of Cong, Co. Mayo in 1952. It was a location which was selected by Lord Killinan who was a friend of the producer.

A beautifully filmed story (similar to Shakespeare's ***Much Ado about Nothing***) of a boxer (John Wayne) who comes home to Inisfree to marry his sweetheart (Maureen O'Hara) much to the chagrin of her brother (Victor McLaglen). It also features the legendary Barry Fitzgerald the first Irish actor to win an Oscar. A tale of repatriation, it never aspired to more than a colourful sentimental romp.

Many myths surround the making of ***The Quiet Man***. The story goes that when setting up for a shoot, the camera crew noticed that one of the houses in the background stood out because the walls were painted bright pink. An envoy was dispatched to offer the owner a handsome sum of money just to paint the cottage white for the film. An obliging woman, she was very happy to do so. The only problem then, was when the crew returned after the weekend to complete the scene, hers was the only whitewashed cottage. All the others were now painted bright pink!

Notwithstanding these setbacks the film took six weeks to complete and much to the delight of Bord Fáilte the weather stayed fine for the shooting. It was beautifully filmed in full technicolour. It was a case of matching lush Irish exteriors where most of the action takes place with interiors shot in studio back in America.

It was a major box office success garnering Ford his sixth Academy Award as Best Director and helping to promote the image of Ireland's natural beauty world-wide. It received six Oscar nominations, winning two and achieved the Best Colour Cinematography trophy. It can be described as a true classic because it has stood the test of time. We'll leave the last – admirably 'stage Irish' – line to Will Danaher:

'He'll regret it till his dying day, if ever he lives that long.'

Following the worldwide success of The Quiet Man, John Ford made a second Irish film in Co. Clare in 1956. It was called **Three leaves of a Shamrock** produced by Lord Killanin, later released under the title **The Rising of the Moon**. It featured the top Abbey actors of the day including Cyril Cusack, Jimmy O'Dea, Maureen Potter, Donal Donnelly, Noel Purcell and Eileen Crowe. This charming trilogy is now a perennial feature on television every St Patrick's day.

Notwithstanding ongoing difficulties, the comings and goings of the film industry people were important to places like Bray and Dublin both from a social and economic viewpoint. For the duration of the filming of **Captain Lightfoot** (1955), Rock Hudson and Barbara Rush stayed at the Tonga suite in The Shelbourne Hotel for a full four months. Neither had a reputation for being generous with tips so it was a surprise on the last night for the hotel staff to be summoned to that same Tonga Suite for their 'going away gifts.' The staff were somewhat underwhelmed with each being personally presented with a signed photograph of the Hollywood stars.

Dublin born Maureen O'Hara was Ireland's leading

Hollywood lady of the 50s. A fine actress with flaming red hair, classic high cheekbones and lightly freckled skin, she was rightly considered one of the most beautiful women in Hollywood. She had made her film debut in *Jamacia Inn* (1939) opposite Charles Laughton. So good was she in that film that she was brought to America to play the leading lady in RKO's epic *The Hunchback of Notre Dame*. The outbreak of World War II stalled her film career and return to Ireland but she eventually came good with some classics such as *How Green Was my valley* (1941) and the *Black Swan* (1942). She worked with the top film directors including Alfred Hitchcock and John Ford but her greatest success was surely her wonderful feisty performance as Mary Kate Danaher in *The Quiet Man*. It was the first time her beauty was captured in Technicolor. Her leading opposites were the from top drawer of Hollywood talent at the time but her favourite leading man was John Wayne, with whom she played in five films between 1950 and 1970. John Ford described her as 'the best bloody actress in Hollywood.'

According to her own autobiography *Tis Herself*, a key defining moment for the young actress was when she finally stood up to the dominant film director John Ford – who'd been nagging her about squinting when her hair blew in her eyes – with the immortal lines:

'What would a baldy-headed old son of a bitch like you know about hair lashing across your eyeballs?'

She had a wonderfully successful career spanning six decades culminating in *The Last Dance* (2000).

The international success of *The Quiet Man* not only delivered Bord Fáilte's dreams in tourist numbers but gave rise to Ireland being used as a non-Irish location as in *Moby Dick* (1956) starring Gregory Peck as Captain Ahab and the port of Youghal starring as New Bedford, Massachusetts. Other films of this period included *Knights of the Round Table* (1953) an early Camelot featuring Robert Taylor and Eva Gardener, Douglas Sirk's *Captain Lightfoot* (1955) featuring Rock Hudson and filmed at Clougherhead, Co. Louth and *Jacquline* (1956), all of which featured the familiar grey bearded Dubliner, Noel Purcell who had an established niche in lesser roles. Muriel Box became the first woman to direct an Irish feature film with *This Other Eden* (1959) which was produced by Emmet Dalton and featuring Milo O'Shea and Hilton Edwards. Although not widely known, Alfred Hitchcock shot one of his early films in Ireland – a complete lemon: *Juno and the Paycock* featuring Sara Allgood, a well known Irish actress. Nobody was impressed, not least the play's author Sean O'Casey.

When Ardmore Studios in Bray, Co. Wicklow were finally established in May 1958, the first big budget film made there was **Shake Hands with the Devil** starring James Cagney trying to save ould' Ireland. Alongside Cagney was an excellent cast made up of the cream of American and British actors including the lovely Dana Wynter, Glynis Johns, Sybil Thorndike and Michael Redgrave. These were supported by young Irish actors including Richard Harris, Cyril Cusack and TP McKenna.

For this writer meeting Dana Wynter in Bray in the early1980s – when she was in RTÉ's *Bracken* with a youthful Gabriel Byrne – was a privilege and a pleasure. Having first come to Ireland for **Shake Hands with the Devil**, she was already an established and enduring actress, having starred in such films as **Invasion of the Body Snatchers** (1956), **D-Day the Sixth of June** (1956), and **Love and War** (1958). She was also a superb writer, contributing to *The Irish Times* and *The Guardian* and her memoir *Other People, Other Places* was published in 2005.

Although Ardmore has played a strong (if intermittent) role in the Irish film industry with over 100 feature films produced there, the studios never really took off to have what could be described as a golden era. From the beginning there were difficulties with unions regarding British and Irish labour, as the only local input came from construction work and catering. Financial difficulties were soon to follow and these were to constantly dog the studios in the years to come, resulting in several liquidations.

For the making of **Rooney** in 1957, the GAA had given permission to Rank to shook the key scenes in Croke Park on All Ireland Hurling Final day. John Gregson, a fictitious Dublin dustman and star hurler was the unlikely hero alongside Barry Fitzgerald and Noel Purcell. The players from Waterford and Kilkenny each received £5 for their cooperation. When the Kilkenny captain Michael Kelly scored the spectacular winning point, it was all over. Alas, some things never change.

Domestically, Gael Linn with its **Amharc Éireann** series had huge success both commercially and culturally with their films from 1956, but particularly George Morrrison's **Mise Éire** in 1959, a trilogy of documentaries telling the history of Ireland from the dawn of time and underscored by the beautiful music of Sean Ó Riada.

Into the late 1960s, it was fortuitous that many famous film directors chose Ireland as home and their influence was positive and profound in the succeeding years. John Huston first visited Ireland in 1951 before becoming an Irish citizen and purchasing a Georgian home in Co. Galway. Similarly, John Boorman came to live in Annamoe, Co. Wicklow in the 1960s and his involvement with Ardmore Studios and the Irish film industry is legendary.

The Roll of Honour – The Top Ten Films at The Stella

THE BORRISOKANE OSCARS

In box office terms, the following 'Boscars' were the
most successful films shown at
the Stella :

FILM TITLE	DATE	FEATURING	GROSS
Guns Of Naverone	1962	Gregory Peck David Niven Anthony Quin Richard Harris	£46-3s-6d
South Pacific	1965	Mitzi Gaynor Rossano Brazzi Joan Kerr	£35-3s

FILM TITLE	DATE	FEATURING	GROSS
The Longest Day (B&W)	1965	John Wayne Robert Mitchum Henry Fonda Robert Wagner Sean Connery Christopher Lee Robert Ryan Rod Steiger & just about everyone.	£28-18s
The Robe	1961	Richard Burton Jean Simmons Victor Mature Michael Rennie	£26-10s
Little Nellie Kelly (B&W)	1958	Judy Garland	£24-1s-6d
Bridge on the River Kwai	1964	Alec Guinness William Holden	£22-7s-6d
The Geisha Boy	1957	Gerry Lewis	£22-1s
Stalig 17 (B&W)	1962	William Holden Don Taylor	£20-17-6d
Song of Bernadette (B&W)	1960	Jennifer Jones Gladys Cooper Vincent Price Lee J Cobb	£18-2s-6d
The Bowrey Boys (B&W)	1957	Jack Hawkins	£16-11s

Harold Lloyd's World of Comedy shown in 1964 was voted the funniest film ever screened at the Stella. It was an assortment of all Lloyd's films including the famous scene where he hangs on for dear life from the hands of a clock in *Safety Last*.

Worst film with best title was *Fire Maidens from Outer Space* (1956).

The cinema archives indicate that the British actor James Mason made more individual appearances than anyone else during the Stella's ten year reign – 28 in all. His performance as an addicted school teacher in *Bigger Than Life* (1953) was a highlight.

In purely educational terms it was felt that the film *Operation Eichmann* shown in 1963 introduced subject matter hitherto unknown to local schoolchildren.

The Dawn was shown in 1964 and had a brief effect on the more ardent nationalists among the young folk.

Louis Marcus's *The Christy Ring Story* shown in 1965 proved very popular, the subject matter being of vital interest locally, as the hurling legend himself only retired in 1967. The Stella archives are set out in an exquisite hand covered ledger held by the late Paddy Heenan, trustee. This consists of each film shown, the date and the door receipts, meticulously kept in the neatest handwriting for the full tenure of the project.

THE LAST PICTURE SHOW

The mid 60s brought with it unprecedented change throughout Ireland in both social and economic terms. In social terms alone, the 60s was to become a truly musical decade with Elvis and the Beatles achieving virtual world domination. The pace of modernism in Ireland was astonishing and no area of life was untouched. Free second level education was introduced in 1967, sowing the seeds of future prosperity. The author of this book was thus among the first class ever of the Borrisokane Vocational School (under the inspirational leadership of principal Dermot Dunne) to sit the Intermediate Cert exam in their own town in 1969. It was also the pinnacle of the Sean Lemass/TK Whittaker era of economic growth. For the first time in generations, emigration was not the only option as the prospect of sustained improvements in living standards at home became a reality.

Between 1960 and 1967, over 350 foreign companies set up in Ireland attracted by generous tax allowances and grants resulting in an unprecedented boom. Shannon Free Airport industrial complex was established and Bord na Móna production was at an all-time high. Locally, the Silvermines which had began mining operations in 1957 – in the same year as the Stella – were now in full production, employing more than 500 people in well paid jobs. Ireland became a serious holiday destination and this was reflected in the number of hollywood legends who chose Ireland for the family holiday. Thus, Charlie Chaplin was a regular in Waterville Co. Kerry where he would go fishing with his friend Walt Disney. In Puckane in Tipperary, Gene Kelly became almost a local in Kennedy's pub annually. By the late 60s the standard of living had doubled. All of this was reflected in social terms with more spending power and travel for young people in particular, the music was everywhere and changed everything. Carnival dances featuring show-bands were in full swing and it was considered nothing for young people from Borris to travel to Moate, Drumkeen or wherever the action was.

In America, a young man had inspired the hopes of the West. President John F Kennedy was a mere kid compared with the worlds elder statement such as Khrushev, Adenaur and De Gaulle. And he was Irish – well sort of – he was considered an American Irishman who was proud of his Irish roots. What did matter was that he had made it to the top of the world, acknowledged his Irishness and that gave us a kind of a glow at the time. The defining moment in the life of the Stella kids (as elsewhere) was the feeling of the end of innocence at the manner and shock of his death. Nearly everyone over 50 years old can to this day remember exactly where they were when they first heard the awful news. In the days that followed, we became engrossed in the whole affair through the new medium of television. The Stella kids stared in awe at the TV set in Slevin's shop window at JFK's seemingly endless military funeral, being particularly impressed by the riderless horse with a pair of boots reversed in the stirrups. Maybe those guns we loved so much on the silver screen were not harmless after all.

The Stella soldiered on bravely but in terms of its life and survival there was now a much more significant threat ... television. In 1960, Slevin Electrical's 60 feet high aerial almost overnight became the tallest feature at that end of the town. RTÉ came into being on New Year's Eve in 1961. In the beginning most people would rent a set rather than commit to buying what was after all a new innovation. The jingle was heard night and day across the land:

If you want TV trouble free, rent a set from RTV, cos RTV have the sets and the service, so rent from RTV.

Television was as revolutionary in cultural terms as the boom was in economic terms. The old order was to change forever. The R.T.E cameras rolled to nearby Shinrone to do a feature on life in 'Our Village'. One elderly farmer was interviewed to ascertain what he thought of the new media. 'Not much,' he declared. 'That fella Gay Byrne above on the Late Late Show ...

Talking to Wimmin, that's all he's good for!' But despite isolated pockets of resistance, reactionary or otherwise, television was to attain a firm grip on Irish life.

Households where animated chatter had defined the family evening meal now fell silent before the powerful new medium. The set was turned on a good hour before broadcast, leaving family members to contemplate every aspect of the so familiar, static St Brigid's cross logo. It was not turned off until after the national anthem, everyone present lingering a few seconds to watch the screen finally disappear into a tiny dot of light. Across Ireland, the traditional verbal culture gave way to a silent one as television held sway. The sets even began to appear behind the counters of the local pubs, to a reverential hush along the counter as banter was confined to the ad breaks. Problems which were never discussed in company and had been swept under the carpet for years were now in the open domain of public discussion. This was the time of the well documented 'bishop and the nightie' affair on the Late Late Show, when a bishop in the west of Ireland took issue with some innocuous chat on the programme. Irish society was changing and television was to the forefront with its influence on young people.

The president of Ireland, Eamon De Valera believed it could be a force for good but worried about its potential for moral harm. He believed it would erode the unique culture of the nation and in his first broadcast stated: 'I must admit that when I think of Television and Radio and their immense power ... I feel somewhat afraid.' Reactionary politicians like Fine Gael's Oliver J.

Flanangan were quoted as saying, 'there was no sex in Ireland before television.'

These were now voices of the past, literally crying in the wilderness. Such was the impact of TV that in year's to come, old people would gaze in nostalgia at TV screens as they reviewed the big events of the 20th Century. And they would remember fondly what they were doing as these historical events were unfolding. Yes, they were watching TV.

It took another few years for TV to impact on Borris but the age of television had arrived permanently and this was to gradually spell the death knell of rural cinema. The cinemas began to close one by one, turning into bingo halls or just plain dereliction. There was a poignancy as these former pleasure palaces were reduced slowly to 'has-been' flea pits. Nationally cinema-going numbers were falling with the exception of Dublin City, which had been Europe's cinema capital for many postwar years with even an active black market for tickets. Although no figures are available nationally the official statistics from the UK tell their own story.

1957 No. of Cinemas 4500 Attendances 25 Million per week
1967 No. of Cinemas 1800 Attendances 9 Million per week

As the number of cinemas decreased, the industry stopped producing blockbusters and rolled out cheaper and poorer films in greater volumes further shrinking the audience. The Stella struggled on for a few more years,

1965 being the first year it actually lost money. Ned Molloy had passed away prematurely, being replaced by Billy Brooks as hall caretaker. It was not destined to outlive its Dublin namesake, Tony O'Grady's Stella Cinema in Rathmines which opened its doors in 1923 and was still doing business 80 years on in 2003.

Early in 1967 some tough decisions had to be taken. There were now more people on the two Bingo buses leaving Church Road for Portumna and Nenagh than there were supporting the little cinema. There was internal discussion amongst the committee as to the best course of action. It would be a big decision to make. They knew if the cinema closed, it would be closed for good. One summer's evening there was a total of 14 patrons in the hall leading to an animated debate amongst the long serving ticket collectors in the foyer. Not all were in agreement. One individual noted for his professional selling skills and less reticent than the rest was clear in his views declaring

'Its over lads, I tell you the writing is on the wall and when that baldy little cleric comes around … (*Enter the Dean*) … Oh good evening Dean, do you know we were just talking about you. How're tings?'

The Dean gave a wry smile not indicating whether he had heard the first part of the conversation but shortly after this a final decision on the old dream palace was taken. On a far greater scale than either 'Stellas', was the Stella cinema on Deerpark Road, Mount Merrion Dublin which opened its doors in July 1954. Initially a tall purpose built screen cinema, it thrived in the 50s and 60s. Finally being run by a staff of two before its closure in 1976. Over two thirds of the homes in the area now had a television set. Rapid and radical change was sweeping the world as undreamed of achievements became almost commonplace via television. A doctor called Christian Bernard had successfully transplanted a heart from one patient to another. There was even talk of landing a man to walk the surface of the moon ... imagine. In Borris, the kids who had packed the front rows in 1957 were now the teenagers of the 60s and their young brothers and sisters were at home in deep space, glued to *The Fugitive, The Man From U.N.C.L.E* or *Quenten Vale of The Everglades* on TV. The world was at their fingertips and another push of a button brought pop music from pirate radio stations such as Radio Caroline.

Unlike urban cinema, the Stella never developed a boyfriend/girlfriend culture probably because you would bring your partner there only if you wanted to let the whole town know of your romantic endeavours. For a 'bit of a court' (romance) you would be better off on the Green Lane. This was after all the 'Summer of Love' on the West Coast of America. 'Flower Power' in Borrisokane consisted of a fella with a daisy over his left ear feeling good as he walked hand in hand with the girl of his dreams. Although drink of the black variety was the only known recreational drug in North Tipp, that feeling of 'something happening' was like a magnet and it wasn't tugging us towards the cinema. The two big pop music hits of 1967 were 'Knights in White

Satin' by the Moody Blues and 'A Whiter Shade of Pale' by Procol Harem. What were theses songs all about? Apparently, 'Knights in White Satin' was inspired by astronauts in their white suits. But 'Whiter Shade of Pale' (apart from 'the light fandango') must remain a mystery and in a way it summed up everything that year. We sang it flying past the dormant cinema on our bikes going home from the 'Tech'. We had all the lyrics but hadn't the foggiest clue what the song was about. It mattered not.

With our hair beginning to grow a bit out over the ears and a cigarette stuck in our gobs we felt we too were somehow 'with it.'

DARRYL F. ZANUCK (U.S.A.) P. LIVINGSTONE
CHAIRMAN MANAGING DIRECTOR

TWENTIETH CENTURY-FOX FILM COMPANY LTD

HEAD OFFICE: TWENTIETH CENTURY HOUSE, SOHO SQUARE, LONDON, W.1
TELEPHONE: GERRARD 7766 TELEX NO. 27869 GRAMS: CENTFOX LONDON TELEX
CABLES: CENTFOX, LONDON, W.1.

14th June, 1967.

Mr. P. J. Heenan,
Stella Cinema,
Borrisokane,
Co. Tipperary,

Dear Sir,

CANCELLATION OF LICENCE AGREEMENTS

This letter confirms that the Licence Agreement made between us in respect of the undermentioned films is hereby cancelled:

STELLA - BORRISOKANE

THE COMANCHEROS		Licence Agreement No.
ASSIGNMENT PHILLIPINES	1 day	2429 dated 30.1.65 and
THE JUMPING HORSE	4.6.67.	Amendments dated 20.10.65
DRUM ROLL		and 29.12.65.
SECOND TIME AROUND		Licence Agreement No.2429
THE FIRST FAST MAIL	1 day	dated 30.1.65 and Amendments
THE GOOD SERVANT	11.6.67.	dated 29.12.65 and 12.3.66.
TENDER IS THE NIGHT	1 day	)
BANANA BINGE	18.6.67	)
		)
STATE FAIR	1 day	)
CROSSING THE DELAWARE	25.6.67.	)
		)
WILD IN THE COUNTRY		) Licence Agreements No. 2429
AUSTRALIAN WATER SPORTS	1 day	) dated 30.1.65 and Amend-
HOUSE OF HASHIMOTO	2.7.67	) ments dated 29.12.65.
		)
THE INSPECTOR		)
ASSIGNMENT PAKISTAN	1 day	)
SAPPY NEW YEAR	9.7.67	)
		)
MR. HOBBS TAKES A VACATION		)
SOUND OF ARIZONA	1 day	)
REALLY BIG ACT	16.7.67	)

Cont../2

CURTAIN CALL
1967

Nineteen Sixty-seven was a landmark year in film. The big Oscar winner was **Bonnie & Clyde**, a film that had it all – tension, violence, love, greed, romance and excitement. Warren Beatty and Faye Dunway, its 'anti-heroes' could simultaneously be worshipped and despised and to cap it all, the film culminated in the mother of all shoot-outs. Set during the Depression, it picked up on the anti-authority, anti-Vietnam War sentiment of 1967. Although at the time many film critics dismissed it as a gory thriller, Pauline Kael, the famous film critic of the *New Yorker* magazine, described it as 'the most excitedly American movie since **The Manchurian Candidate**.'

Jane Fonda's mini-skirted legs were the best feature of **Barefoot In The Park** and ladies, who was that gorgous blonde hunk - none other than Robert Redford. Sidney Poitier and Rod Steiger sizzled **In the Heat of the Night** with similar racial themes trotted out in **Guess Who's Coming to Dinner** the latter film was more like a stage play with Spencer Tracey and Katharine Hepburn as the parents in their last film together. Dustin Hoffman became an overnight success in his debut film *The Graduate* helped along by the music of Simon & Garfunkel. The Duke was still making Westerns, this time alongside Robert Mitchum – playing himself? – as a drunk, in *El Dorado*. Paul Newman found himself at the wrong end of a prison guard's boot in *Cool Hand Luke* which gave us one of the great film understatements, 'What we got here ... is a failure to communicate.' British actors Peter Cook and Dudley Moore starred in the Faustian cult film *Bedazzled,* proving that there were plenty of lemons' made that year too.

Francis Ford Copolla was cutting his directorial teeth with the stage-Irish *Finian's Rainbow*. Wicklow director John Boorman's thriller *Point Blank* was a good as any film made that year. Worst film of the year just had to be Roman Polansky's *Valley of The Dolls*. Leading actress Jayne Mansfield was beheaded in a car crash, not long after her controversial visit to Tralee. Martin Sheen starred alongside Beau Bridges in his first film *The Incident* shot in grainy black and white with noticeably poor sound.

It was also the year that Mel Brooks created his first film *The Producers*. It featured Gene Wilder as a mild mannered accountant who teams up with a has-been Broadway impresario Zero Mostel, to stage a musical called 'Springtime for Hitler'. This was to be a contrived failure, a vehicle to swindle little old ladies out of their money. Brilliantly original and hilariously funny at the time it has not dated well. Unfortunately in the very month it opened in Dublin, the final curtain had just fallen at the Stella. Curiously enough, 1967 was the year Jammet's French restaurant in Nassau Street Dublin also closed down. This had been an oasis in the city for over 60 years for visiting film stars such as Rock Hudson, Elizabeth Taylor, Bing Crosby and Rod Steiger.

The Stella Cinema closed in May 1967, more with a whimper than the bang with which it had opened ten years earlier, as hardly anyone noticed. The last film shown in the Stella was certainly not in the proud tradition of the old cinema in that it was a national road safety film for schoolchildren. This time there would be no fanfare. The projector was sold to Duffy's Circus, the screen dismantled and the hall reverted to its original usage, the odd play or meeting and a permanent place of residence for old celluloid ghosts. It was not destined to outlive either of its Dublin namesakes such as the Stella Cinema in Mount Merrion which started the same year but lasted until 1976.

However its fair to say that it had made its mark. In the words of the late great Peter Sellers (as he dragged himself from a marsh in *A Shot in the Dark*), 'It was all part of life's rich pageant'. Like any mass media it created myths for its own agenda and downright lies for general consumption. There is very little that is heroic about cowboys or war. However, cinema is an art form and perhaps it was this medium that Pablo Picasso had in mind when he said: 'Art is the lie that enables us to realise the truth.' It certainly created an enormous impact in its time. As the ultimate 'time machine', it rendered a small victory for idyllic fantasy over harsh reality, it brought exposure to a different culture, mainly that of America. Who knows, maybe it was a precursor to the day when the next generation would travel on trains in Irish cities speaking Americanese – Hi! Like OK Guys, Like Roight!, Hello! – on their mobile phones to their friends. To be fair, it had brought music and colour, mystery and magic, information and education, joy and excitement during a drab period in our country's social and economic history. Although a refuge from reality, in its own way it was also the catalyst for change with the sheer sorcery of cinema, the local became the universal. All in all it was a tremendous facility, ahead of its time in a little Irish town and the smooth professional running of the cinema underlined the ten year commitment of a small number of local people. Their motive was love, not greed or profit. Week in, week out, they gave unselfishly, their time as an example of community service at its best. If nothing else, this little book is a belated tribute to those people – the real stars. 'Thank You' from the people of Borris and district who had great pleasure enjoying the magic of the Stella for so long.

The Magnificent Seven–
Downtown Desperados

QUACKSER

Quackser leaned against the side of Heenan's gateway, puffing the earthly remains of his 'Woodbine' cigarette and watching the world go by. The archway was a good vantage point, being in the middle of the street. A handy place to park a bike. From where he stood, he could just make out the strains of Miss Guilfoyle's wireless belting out Elvis: 'Return to Sender ... Address unknown'. Number One in this weeks Top-Ten. As he hums along to the tune he muses, 'Surely Miss Guilfoyle is not an Elvis fan! But, be-God, you'd never know now. This is 1962 after all. Modern times man!'

Quackser considered himself a man of the world – Brylcreem man. Twelve years old but a fully-fledged member of the 'Downtowns'. Small for his age, but when he swaggered down the street with the gang he felt about ten feet tall. 'Where the hell were they anyway?'

It was well past 7.30 and Tom Kelly had gone down the street behind his cows ages ago. The last of the stragglers had passed up from evening devotions, so why the delay? Tonight was Wednesday night and that meant only one thing – the pictures at the Stella, down on Mill Street. Though he couldn't have seen that many films in his short lifetime, he considered himself something of a buff. He was a born earwigger – a good listener and was quick to pick up on the key items in any discussion, particularly on film. This added immensely to his supposed repertoire and the range of films he had seen. In fact, he was never known to admit to not having seen a film under discussion. More bluff than buff. Once, in a moment of animated conversation, he actually claimed to have been an extra in *Captain Lightfoot*, filmed while he was on his holidays in Bray. ('Now there's one for the books lads, wha'). However, he had to refute this dubious claim for lack of evidence when challenged. It was a mistake. He knew that his credibility was dented for a while. Nevertheless, his enthusiasm and grasp of the subject was beyond question and his surface knowledge impressive for his tender years.

For all his urbanity and sociability the primal call of nature was strong within him and the need for solitude drew him back to the river. As a lad ever keen to escape reality (harsh or otherwise) the medium of film was most suitable to him. He was shy, sensitive and considered a bit of an oddball due to a complete lack of interest in sport. When he walked down Main Street, he felt the eyes of the town were on him alone. He knew from school that God was everywhere (omnipresent) and could see all things. Between God and neighbours behind 'squinting windows,' was there to be any escape? Would he go stone mad? He loved his verdant terrain which he had walked since he learned how to walk. Every tree, stone and bush was a significant milestone. He loved to mitch from school, just to go fishing down by the sluice gates at Breretons. Sitting with rod and line where the waters narrowed to a frothy chasm over a deep pool, he felt truly alone. One could sit there for hours under a bush, totally out of sight. He would watch the dippers glide in, grey wagtails hop across the stones and if lucky, the blue flash of the kingfisher winging his way under the trees. The water had a hypnotic calming effect on him and inspired him to poetry, the only subject that interested him at school. What would the poet have made of it all.

> I went out to the hazel wood,
> because a fire was in my head.
> I dropped the berry in the stream,
> and caught a little silver trout.
> — W.B. Yeats

'Poetry and ould films,' his father would say, 'won't get you far in this world, me boy.' To which Mother would add her party-piece on cue, 'You'd be better off doing the nine first Fridays, for your future son.' But Quackser wasn't interested. From a steady diet of films at that impressionable age, he had begun a process of believing in all things American. He thought of America as the land of opportunity. It was full of winners, cheeky chancers (not unlike himself), wisecracking villains, husky blondes and garrulous cops, all living amidst glowing prosperity. He couldn't help making the comparisons between American film families and his own crowd. The American model won handsomely. The kids looked rich and some of them were on first name terms with their young and handsome parents. They had everything from tree-houses to comfortable shoes (which they called 'sneakers') contrasting sadly with his own hobnailed boots. He took a mental note that he must get to this place called America as soon as he can. He thought of American fathers going on vacation to exciting places like the Catskills or going fishing with their kids. He thought of his own Dad at home reading the paper and grumbling about the state of the world. He was like a gramophone stuck in its groove.

'Poetry! Some days I think that lad is turning into a right gobshite.' Quackser did have one redeeming quality. He was a good listener. He would sit on the bridge and listen to the men in the peaked caps tell their tall tales. His ears went back like a hare for any stories concerning film or cinema. He had the knack of absorbing the keys points in any story and retelling them, further embellished by his own little additions. He could put a 'skin' on any story.

His all-time favourite story was about the man who went into the 'Mars' Cinema in Kilrush, Co. Clare. Apparently, after taking his seat he looked around and was astounded to see a dog sitting in a seat beside its owner. During the interval he brought this to the attention of the cinema manager. 'Ah that's only Patch, no bother there at all. Just watch.'

On observing the dog for the second half, he was amazed to note that the dog seemed to be actually watching the film. During the scary bits he would cower in the seat and during the happy bits he would wag his tail. At the end he was so impressed that he went over to the old man.

'I must commend your dog there. Contrary to what I thought, he seemed to be really interested in the film.' The old man put down his pipe, 'Faith he was surely, and strange to say, he didn't like the book one bit all.'

Our Quackser was a great man to absorb and repeat the banter all right, and sometimes, even when he told the truth, he could tell even better stories. It was not so much that he told outright lies, but he did render a bit of modification to the truth in order to give it more colour and vitality. But its surely time now for him to head to the picture house with or without his pals. With one final glance towards the sky he neatly puts out his Woodbine and pockets it for later on as he heads on down towards the Stella.

ALMANAC

Almanac could never really fathom the nickname. He had picked it up in school on the day he read aloud that dreadful composition about the seasons in English class. But the name stuck anyway. His friends called him Al, the tallest of the mob. He didn't have much by the way of personality so instead he became a collector. He had a master collection of bottles, comics, old watches, annuals and tin soldiers. He even collected car registration numbers and could be seen after school most days looking very serious, as he licked the end of his pencil and jotted car numbers into his little note book. He would cross check the book every week, extract duplicate numbers to discover he had AFI 665 for perhaps the third time. A harmless occupation, until once he got too close to the half open boot of a farmer's station-wagon. For more street-wise boys, the loosely arranged straw would have given some clue but

Almanac was too wrapped up in his numbers. As he got closer to try and make out the mud splattered number plate, he was damn near savaged to death by Mickey Keenan's mad greyhound bitch. She lived there with her pups and did not welcome visitors. He gave up the numbers racket after this but dogs seemed to become the bane of his life.

Al was practical and on Wednesday nights he busied himself about the house, to ensure (not that there was ever much doubt) that his mother would come good with the money for himself and his kid brother 'Joey' to get to the pictures. He cleaned, dusted, cleared out the turf shed and offered to whitewash, for only the third time since Easter.

Big Al was manly if anything. Beyond the greyhound incident, the only shadow on his reputation for coolness under pressure concerned the horror film **Captain Clegg**. Mother had heard that this was a Hammer film (in fact its US title was **Night Creatures**) and she was dubious. But Al assured her in his usual suave style that there would not be a problem. Of course he got to go, on the basis that he would mind little Joey the brother and protect him from any fright. In the cinema things were going just fine at the beginning. The usual Wednesday crowd were all in. Glancing back up towards the plush seats he could see the red glow in the dark and the familiar cloud of blue smoke as Cissie puffed her way through the show, horror films being her particular favourite. He kept a protective eye on young Joey who sat unperturbed through the early stages of the film. Suddenly, one of Captain Clegg's victims (a harmless servant who had been beheaded early on) made an unscheduled reappearance fresh from his coffin, bearing his severed head on a silver tray. This was too much for our Al even though little brother was still grinning throughout. He was petrified – he made a charge for the cinema door, dragging young Joey along with him. Poor Jimmy in the foyer got a bigger fright as two kids nearly broke down the front door in the panic to escape.

Down past Guilfoyle's overhanging trees they scurried. How threatening they now looked in the moonlight, more like a mango swamp – not going under those tonight. Across the road to the Mill side. Quite suddenly, 'Tailor' Horrigan – a mongrel of ill-repute, well known for his capacity to make rapid adjustments to boy's clothing with his teeth – releases a blood-curdling howl.

'My God!' Stick to the middle of the road, past the old Mill – right at the corner and away up the hill, getting there, panting. At long last – home sweet home. In the front gate dragging the young fella after him, catching a few deep breaths. Turn the handle and into the hall, quickly bolting the front door behind him. Now for the silent sneak up the stairs while gagging little Joey. So far so good. Into his familiar bedroom. Try to sleep, but the curtains just won't go fully across. Wondering about that dead bat he found in the garden last week, his poor mind is working overtime. Another blood curdling howl from 'Tailor' – 'Christ!' He's under the window this time and Al bolts out of his bed.

'Mam can I talk to you for a minute?'

Mother knew the score at this stage and our brave Al finally got to sleep safe and sound in Mother's bed that night. The only redeeming feature was that none of the gang would know of this escapade, once he had bribed little Joey. A weeks supply of sweets might do the trick. That was last Wednesday and tonight Al has decided to stay in and give the pictures a rest. His secret was safe for now, but you can't be too careful in this town he had decided, as he kept one eye on Joey chewing his sweets in the corner.

BOSCO

Bosco was smart, a cute hoor altogether. He kind of stood out. With his apple jaws and sandy hair and freckles, he looked different. He was clever and wary of any one who seemed more clever than he. He had something of a dictator's disdain for intellectuals. He was the leader and he brooked no dissent. He could normally depend on the loyalty of Al and Quackser to deter any insurgents. He wouldn't be in Heenan's gateway on Wednesday evenings. The usual routine was when a few had gathered there, they would head towards Bosco's house. Nobody would actually go to the door until Al (the deputy) had gone in. You could have up to ten kids waiting outside the house by times. Inside it was assumed the chosen few were discussing matters of state importance. Inside, Al and Bosco his trusty lieutenants were taking their time finishing a game of cards.

When they did emerge, the full contingent would head towards Mill Street en route to the cinema. Passing Slevin's Radio & Electrical shop, most pretended not to notice the television set on display in the shop window. Three of them were late last week watching *Daithí Lacha* (as Gaeilge) in the window and Bosco the leader was not impressed. It was the most stupid thing he could ever imagine. 'Gobshite of a duck ... can't move ... doesn't even speak English.' He had strong views on TV. 'It'll never catch on lads! Its small, black and white, fuzzy with a picture of the St Brigids cross on display most of the time. Let's face it, I'm a Stella man! There were only three TV sets in the town that he knew of at that time. For a boy of such tender years, he was all convincing that his world view was the only relevant one for the times.

Along Mill Street they went, until they reached Guilfoyle's shop. Here they paused and went in, two by two. Bosco and Al first. The first treats of the evenings entertainment were the 'soups' – a serving of ice-cream in a tin bowl with raspberry syrup on top. Mighty stuff. Potato crisps were new on the scene – Murphy's 'Nukcrisps'. Bosco laughingly warned never, ever, to mix the Nukcrisps and the 'soups'. Quackser was suddenly quiet. He had done just that during the **Guns of Naverone** and developed a dose of the 'runs'. When he hadn't returned from the Gents (after his sixth visit) some of the lads went out to check. Just as well. Quackser was stuck inside the cubicle with the heavy wooden door. The Hall management went into rescue operations, but eventually had to borrow a jemmy to prize the door open. The unfortunate Quackser was released just in time for the end of the film but he stayed off the 'soups' for a while after this.

Bosco had masterminded a system whereby four of them could get in on one ticket. This involved the first one in retaining his ticket, heading for the toilet and handing it out the window to the lads waiting outside. This caper didn't work because on the third night it was tried, the ticket was handed out to the wrong person. The 'Tightner' O'Reilly was parking his bike, having just cycled in from Carney and was delighted to be gifted a ticket from an unknown hand furtively stretching out through the window. Bosco completed a quick head count before entering the cinema. The only one unaccounted for was Banjo but he was keeping a very low profile lately. Unknown to the lads, Banjo was watching them from the top branches of the ancient chestnut tree in the church grounds just across the road from the picture house. What was he doing up there? Well that's another story.

BANJO

Banjo was the loner. Only nine years old, he was just half a head under Al but he was a hard case. Given any bit of encouragement there was nothing he would not try, nowhere he feared to go. He was a qualified 'bog-trotter,' which is not as simple as it sounds. There is a particular skill and confidence in being able to traverse a bog at high speed. The secret is to keep one's weight on the foot in the air at all times and leap to an unyielding tussock in a split second. He earned his nickname because like his brother Flann and all his family he was musical. This aspect came to light early on in his school career. A temporary teacher in the school was so pleased with Banjo's singing voice and his mastery of the scales that she left him in charge of the junior infant's class for an hour. Taking his job seriously, he decided to teach the class a song or two to put down the time. When

Miss Haran returned, the whole class proudly sang 'The Congo Song', a local composition which they had just learned word for word from Banjo.

> Will you come to the Congo, will you come ?
> Bring your own ammunition and your gun,
> You'll be lying on the grass with an arrow in your ass,
> Will you come to the Congo, will you come?

Banjo was not asked to mind the junior infants after this. He had bundles of energy and was always looking for an outlet for his talents. One of these was his wonderful ability to spit. He had a little gap between his front teeth which was designer fashioned for the short spit at any angle. However, it was in the long distance spit events that Banjo was the specialist. In a final decider in the Laurels, Banjo completed a measured and recorded spit of 24ft – the full width of the river. Granted, the wind was in his favour and he took a great run up to it. There was a spontaneous outburst of applause from the assembled boys as the 'gollier' sailed high across the river finally settling on the wall at the far side. The spot on the wall was treated with awe for some time thereafter, as his record was never broken. He was a natural tree climber and could not only emulate Tarzan, but the apes as well, swinging from tree to tree. The trouble Banjo had with the gang was that he would never 'die' after being fairly shot. He always claimed the bullet had winged him or simply missed but the rules were laid down, when you're shot you die, fair and simple. He had the added distinction of having his name carved on every pew in the church.

Banjo's most notorious exploit which became known as the 'catapult' affair, was to become the talk of the town for weeks. It was during a film called ***Three Coins in the Fountain***, which was on during chestnut season. A real tearjerker for the ladies – definitely a two hanky job. As usual, he paid his 6d for his hard seat in the second row. In fairness, at the door it was pointed out that this film might not exactly be to his taste but the cinema was half full so he went on in anyway. As was his norm, he wormed his way back to the 'dear' seats during the Pathe News. But the film bored him, all romance and talk.

The honeyed lyrics of theme song was an ominous early warning signal:

> Three coins in the fountain,
> Each one seeking happiness,
> Thrown by three hopeful lovers,
> Which one will the fountain bless,
>
> Just one wish will be granted,
> One heart will wear a Valentine.

The dialogue was even worse. The hero started to whine about how his life now seemed so empty and pointless and this film was surely proof that he was right in this regard:

'Oh Jean,' he murmured softly, 'and to think, I never

knew ... and in my life I shall have only this precious moment to remember.'

'By this time tomorrow, my darling Enzio, I will have set sail for the coast of Antiga but I will always remember those times we shared ...'

It was all too much for young Banjo. He began to get edgy and powers beyond himself came into play. He could see the tufty hair on top of Fats Meara's head bobbing up and down at the bottom of the screen and the temptation was overpowering. He had his catapult neatly tucked under his gansey and a shiny chestnut in the pocket of his trousers. Steady ... aim ... fire. There was a distinct crack off Fats' head as the chestnut ricocheted up on to the silver screen. With uncustomary accuracy, the light of the floor manager's torch beamed down and pinpointed Banjo as he froze in his plush seat. The catapult was dropped and his arms were folded as he stared straight at the screen. This was a technique he had perfected in school when he simply didn't have the answers. Strangely, a second light now shone back up at him from the front row. At this stage, the men in the projection room had sensed something was wrong, so the film stopped and the lights went up. Poor Banjo sat there just like James Cagney surrounded by the cops in ***Angels with Dirty Faces***.

Margie in the same row (known as 'three bags a night') momentarily stopped chewing her favourite 'Scots Clan' sweets. The Gauger himself in the back row woke up prematurely to witness the enfolding drama. He usually fell asleep after the ferret competition and did not wake up before the playing of the National Anthem. His head rose quickly, so quickly that he forgot the metal sign – Beware Of Beam When Rising – strategically placed on the wall to his left. His head resounded off the beam as he lurched down again uttering a few unprintable sounds.

Banjo was frog-marched out into the foyer for interrogation. What a grilling.

'For a start what were you doing in the dear seats with your sixpenny ticket?'

'Bringing a weapon into the hall!'

'You're not the Baluba who put the hole in the circular window by any chance?' Banjo played dumb. He thought of himself as the hard man, unbroken even as the tears were welling behind his eyes. He wanted to grit his teeth and say

'You'll never pin this rap on me boys.'

But the words never came. Instead he pleaded the Fifth Amendment – staying silent – just like Cagney until he saw the electric chair. Borris being an easy going town, he was re-admitted quietly, although his trusty catapult was consigned to the boiler furnace. He sat there in silent isolation as the film resumed. But he was livid at having been caught. He had always acted alone but never once broken his eleventh commandment 'Thou shalt not get caught.' He was the prime suspect in many misdemeanors but nothing had ever been proven. It was said he had hidden Pat the Diamond's clothes from the riverbank when Pat was wading through the Meetings, naked as a seal, freeing up one of his nightlines. As

Pat made his way up the Round Hill with just a furze bush to cover his manhood, Banjo was sitting on a wall poking a bit of tar off the road with a stick pretending not to notice. His favourite pastime was tying thread to door knockers and tugging at it from across the street. When the manager of the National Bank made it down three flights of stairs, a face on him like a bag of rusty nails, Banjo was around, but unseen. A cool operator, up to now.

The incident was never mentioned in school, but the nudges and winks said it all. The truth was dawning on Banjo slowly. He had been set up – fingered. Not alone that, but by one of his own so called gang of pals . Even in his trauma, he could recall the smirk on Speckys' face, the smart-ass with the second torch. The swine! Revenge was brewing in his mind and he was not seen in Heenan's gateway on Wednesday evenings. Besides he had plans hatching and key amongst these was getting that Specky fella into his catapult sights. He knew just the spot ...

SPECKY FOUREYES

Specky was the intellectual of the gang. In school, the teacher had described him as 'very individualistic' but the lads weren't sure what this meant and anyway they had their own opinions. He rarely spoke in class but took everything in. Once, during a Geography lesson on rivers, he put his hand up to proffer some obscure information which he had just gleaned.

'Did you know that the male frog when mating, will copulate 500 times in a day. He will cover everything he meets in the river, including shells, old boots and the odd female frog. Could this account for the vast amount of frogspawn visible in our river?'

Now the lesson was Geography, as Biology was light years away. The silence was deafening. The only sound was that of the tuning fork from the junior infants in the next room. The teacher was dumbstruck and muttered something about returning to the rivers of Europe as he faced the blackboard. Clearly teacher training college had not fully prepared him for dealing with young intellectuals.

Specky really loved the pictures, his favourite films being *The Thirty Nine Steps* and *Twelve Angry Men*. He had an enquiring mind and said he could relate to the hero in *Thirty Nine Steps*. But it was anyone's guess what he saw in *Twelve Angry Men*. In this film, Henry Fonda plays the part of a young juror who single-handedly stands up for a young black man accused of murder. Fine and dandy ... but in the opinion of the young blades, it hardly had the vital ingredients for a cracking film, namely shooting (i.e. bullets, arrows or spears), action with fast horses and no oul' kissing or the like. In a word it was not swashbuckling. The whole of *Twelve Angry Men* took place in a courtroom and Bosco led a mass walkout half way through leaving Specky on his own. Bosco often wondered how this lad got into the gang at all. 'No more clockroads after this, lads.'

But Specky knew his own mind regarding the pictures. He had it figured out that Americans were the most honest people in the world . Not only did they not lock their cars in the pictures but they left the keys in as well! What bothered him greatly however was why, when the male lead had finally gotten into a nice compromising position on the casting couch with the beautiful female lead, the phone rang ... always. And guess what, yer man always answered it. Why did American men always wear their hats indoors, even sitting down? This made no sense to a thinking man like Specky.

He was interested in everything and not beyond a bit of divilment either. In the interests of scientific research, he loved to send some of the more innocent lads on the odd 'fools errand.' He had sent Quackser into Lawlor's to ask for a glass hammer. On another occasion he sent young Kennedy into AG Cookes, the chemist. He first explained what MPSI over the chemist shop door meant. It was clearly 'monkey's piss sold inside.' Every schoolboy knew that. So to further young Kennedy's education, he was instructed to ask for a bag of contraceptives in the shop – whatever they were? The pharmacist, obviously trying to be helpful, asked what they were needed for and the first thing that came into Kennedy's head was, 'Indigestion, Sir.' He came out with a box of tablets and as they had been paid for, Specky decided to take three of them anyway. He was overjoyed to discover later that they had the effect of turning his pee a pinky red colour. The word got out in class and the chemists was soon doing a roaring trade in these particular indigestion tablets. They really did work. Bosco remained unimpressed and was waiting for his moment. He made all the appropriate noises in Speckys direction, his favourite film threat line being

'You've just signed your own death warrant buddy, you're a heading for Boot Hill.'

But Specky was having none of this caper, asking to see this death warrant and was it signed up properly. Was it legal?

The following Wednesday night the whole gang were sitting in their usual seats watching the trailer before the big show ***The Guns of Timberland*** featuring Alan Ladd. It was Quackser's birthday and as he was flush with funds, he bought everyone a bottle of 7-Up in Guilfoyles. The projector had broken down and the time honoured practice of stamping on the floor to speed matters up was in full swing. Specky returned from the toilet to catch the restart of the film and took a good swig of his 7-Up bottle. He felt it tasted odd and when he held it up to the light he thought he could detect a faint pinky colour. His worst fears were confirmed when he observed the collective grin along the whole row in response to his query if anyone got a strange taste from their drinks. Bosco had his own way of sorting out anybody smarter than himself! Omertà.

KIPPER

Kipper was Banjo's older brother and was cultivating a pair of 'sidelocks' in his hair to further prove his maturity. An in-between, he was too old for the gang and too young to join the hard chaws in the balcony. Although maturity was not on his side, he was a born romantic. He had first fallen in love with Barbara Stanwyck, star of ***The Cattle Queen of Montana*** and his life would never be the same. However, she belonged to the realm of fantasy and was clearly unavailable. Casting his sights about locally, he had come to fancy Nance, daughter of Tull Toomey, the biggest cattle dealer in town. For decades (it seemed to him) he had watched Nance from afar, without having the courage to approach her. She was beautiful and none of the locals had ever succeeded in getting a date from her. Whether this was snobbery or shyness, was not known but all suitors were turned down.

It could be said that there was a certain apprehension about approaching Tull's house. He was a renowned marksman, despite having one glass eye, he regularly won every clay pigeon prize in the county. It was reputed he could shoot snipe in the dark. He was so keen on this hobby that his kitchen window was constantly ajar. This was so that if an unfortunate magpie or crow flew into his yard as he was breakfasting, Tull was well ready. The gun was positioned in a such a way that he didn't even have to move from his breakfast table. He would fire up into the trees along the front avenue, scattering black and white feathers in all directions. He had seven daughters, one better looking than the next and he had made it known locally that if any young man ever 'took advantage' of any of his brood they might well befall the same fate as the magpies.

It was with some anxiety therefore, that Kipper ambled up along the dark avenue that Wednesday night. He half remembered some wise old saying from a *Tarzan* film, something to the effect that it was 'better not to insult the crocodile's mother before you swim across the river'. He wasn't stupid. But he had succeeded where so many had failed in that he had actually procured a date with the lovely Nance. She would be returning to the convent boarding school after Easter and God alone knows what would happen after that. Kipper had never been so well scrubbed in his life. He had finished off his hair-wash in the barrel outside the back door to take full advantage of the soft rainwater. His only teenage pimple was now invisible under a coating of his sister's talcum powder. He had a bottle of aftershave which had been liberally applied to every nook and cranny in his body including his socks. He certainly looked gallant agreed his mother as she helped put the final cows-lick to his quiff of hair. In the hours before the appointed time he was literally walking on air. He would surely 'shift' tonight. What was that oul' song? 'I have often walked, down that street before ...'

Tull was gone to the mart in Portumna to buy calves, the mud-marks from the tyres of his lorry being the only evidence in the front yard. Nance looked simply gorgeous as she stood in the half light at the front door. He gallantly presented her with the box of chocolates as she took his arm and together they floated back down the avenue towards the cinema. He had timed it so none of the local yobs were hanging around the front railings outside the cinema. Everything was just ... well, perfect.

At the shorts they chatted happily and shared the chocolates. During the Pathe News they cuddled in a bit closer. The main feature began. ***Love me or Leave me*** starring no one he ever heard of before or since. But it was okay. It had mood, music and the dialogue spoke for itself:

'You know, when you were absent, the days seemed like years, and the years seemed like ... Oh daaahling.'

She spoke in a plummy upper class English accent. Yer man was a sailor, supposed to be Swedish or something.

'Abigail, I luff you, promise you'll come vith me ...'

As the couple on-screen commenced their world cruise, Kipper slipped his arm across her slender shoulders ... to no resistance. If there was going to be a 'fly in the ointment', it could only be 'Lurch' Lanigan in the seat behind. Personal hygiene was not Lurch's strong suit but tonight at least he had left his wellingtons at home. He had been working on the bog all day and his mad Aunt Ethel had given him a feed of steak and onions before his weekly treat at the pictures. He emitted one belch during the break which was an ominous early warning signal. A lifetime of Aunt Ethel's greasy steak and a love of dark chocolate had not helped his medical condition, now known as irritable bowl syndrome. Doctor Qually had recommended a dairy free diet but occasionally he 'broke out'. Tonight, during the most poignant and tender moment of *Love me or Leave me*, as the heroine was threatening to fulfil the second promise in the title, Lurch broke wind. To be fair, he was a little conscious of the young pair in front, so it was not exactly a volcanic eruption of seismic proportions of which he was well capable. No, he smuggled this one around the left cheek of his backside, directing it towards the radiator on the wall. Subtle but deadly. The effect was instant. The fall-out seemed to waft along the six rows immediately to the front. Certainly Kipper and the lovely Nance were in the front line of fire. Swiftly and silently, Nancy picked up Kipper's strategically placed left arm and to his eternal dismay resolutely handed it back to him. She shifted at least half a seat away from the perplexed Kipper. A brooding isolation descended.

The atmosphere turned to ice. Lurch had disappeared from his seat behind. Kipper was devastated – too riven with the total injustice of it all – struck dumb! Not a word was spoken, until after the National Anthem when Kipper feebly offered to walk Nance home. With his last fling of the dice he proffered:

'I'm sorry ... about ... earlier.'

She turned her head so that now he could see the resemblance to ould Tull.

'Oh! So it was you ... and me thinking it was that Lurch creature behind us.'

With that she spotted one of her girlfriends and was gone in an instant.

When winds have gathered the sun
and moon behind them,
Above its cloudy rim;
But let a gentle silence wrought with music flow,
whither her footsteps go.
– W.B. Yeats

RED

Red was small of stature with flaming red hair and freckles. By the standards of John Wayne, she was deemed to have **True Grit**. Bony of elbow and knobbly of knee, she was a formidable bundle of raw energy. She could outrun, out-climb, and outsmart most of the lads any day. She had been something of a disciple for ages, until proving her considerable worth and being fully inaugurated into the gang. In front of all, she had demonstrated her commitment by swallowing a live lizard from the bog. Even Maggot Murphy, noted connoisseur of earthworms that he was, had balked at this one. Nobody had even attempted this before. It was just that Bosco had deviously raised the entry stakes (she being a girl) but she had called his bluff that day. There was no argument from then on, she was fully accepted as a valuable gang member. Boys being boys, they were all aspiring to become actors, athletes or failing this, collectors. Red was different. She had a personality. But she also had a great love of cinema and the film world. Not for her the cardboard cut out adventures of the Von Trapp family or the Secret Seven. No. She was in fact an early adherent of method acting and her knowledge of armaments and weapons gave her an inspirational role in the gang's military activities.

What looked to most people like an innocuous lump of wood, in Red's imaginative scheme of things became a bazooka. The leg of a chair could quickly be converted to a belt-fed Gatling machine gun under her expert guidance. **Robin Hood** was her all time favourite. There was nothing she did not know about Sherwood Forest. Consequently, most of her time was spent in the Fort, around the 'big tree' where she could survey the kingdom with her own band of 'merrie men.' She was a born organiser and rallied the lads into mass-production of bows and arrows as quickly as saplings could be cut, hung and dried. There was hardly a stick left in the Fort or a feather left in Mrs Fagan's hen-house. While Red carved out for herself the plum role of Maid Marion, the only reason 'Fats' Fagan got into the gang (briefly) was use of the hen-house and the unflattering role of Friar Tuck. Boys can be cruel at times.

But it was from American and British films that her best ideas came from. In the **Bridge On The River Kwai**, Red was really taken by the machetes used to hack through the thick steamy jungle. She searched the town until she spotted something similar in Lawlor's shop (for topping beet) and so the 'choppers' was born. This implement became a status symbol for the gang and had many uses. With almost cinematic destiny, the choppers reign did come to grief in the end, not only bringing Red down with it but precipitating the break up of the gang.

At the centre of the wood a totem pole had been lovingly erected from a slim beech tree with all the side branches removed. It had been embellished with notches and tribal carvings. For ages it was a focal point for all types of activity including the annual rain dance. But Bosco had laid down a set of complicated rules and regulations. At his whim a guilty party could spend the day tied to the totem pole. Once too often, Red was the routine chosen victim and Bosco's initial mistrust of her was about to be vindicated. Having bribed Banjo, she was freed from her bondage. In a fit of rage, she angrily chopped down the totem pole leaving only a splintered stump at the centre of the holy ground. Red had gone over the top this time and had to make a rapid escape taking the 'choppers' and the now besotted Banjo along with her. The lads were enraged and headed off in hot pursuit. She was last seen heading out the Nash's road and Bosco responded by sealing off all strategic routes back to the town. It became a physiological battle between hunter and hunted, Red wanting the chase as much as Bosco wanted revenge. The offending choppers were hidden under a rain water barrel to rust for years. The vanquished Red and Banjo had effectively gone underground and were nowhere to be seen. Bosco tired of the hunt. In time honoured tradition this war would end at teatime, to resume the following day where it left off. Still, it meant two less punters to meet Quackser at the Wednesday evening rendezvous.

STORM CLOUDS

The storm clouds that had gathered all evening soon turned to rain as darkness descended on the streets. An early roll of thunder had dislodged Banjo from his rookery in the chestnut tree and he opted for the warmth and darkness of the Stella. This time, he occupied the more adolescent realms of the balcony, hand in hand with his girlfriend, Red. His brother Kipper had taken up poetry and long walks by the river to overcome his despondency. Bosco and Al confidently took their traditional places on the outside seats and the single 'Woodbine' cigarette was being passed along the row for a quick drag. Specky was wiping the rain off his glasses in anticipation of a blockbuster. The title of the film was **Key Largo**, which gave little away regarding the plot.

Meanwhile Quackser ambling along the Main Street, had knotted his handkerchief in the corners, placing it on his head as minimal protection against the elements. Torrents of rain descending like the proverbial stair-rods inspiring half remembered rhymes.

'It was raining in the ocean, not a street-car was in

sight. The rain came down in bucketful's, and it rained all day that night.'

The drain channels were fast flowing with brown water as the occasional ice lolly stick made its final journey down to the river. The river itself was tonight a noisy torrent, rushing headlong towards its meeting with the Shannon. There was a familiar lone figure on the bridge. As he passed, he recognised the unsmiling 'Speaker' solitary as a polar bear talking to himself. Perhaps he's had a few too many. Speaker looked up at the young poet, water freewheeling down his grizzled old face.

'And you Gossun, don't stick around this town. Nothing here for you now. Look up that street, will ya. Nothing but telegraph poles. No work here. Hit the high road Jack and pull the door out after you.'

A soaked Quackser wondered earnestly what the old seer was raving about this time. Anyway, he believed he could figure it out later, given that the climatic conditions were not amenable to philosophy, there and then. He turned the corner into a deserted Mill Street. He sheltered a while under the leaky galvanised roof of Tim Heenan's Mill shed. Bags of grain were piled almost to the ceiling but he found a dry corner and struck a match. Visibility was poor but he could just make out the outline of the Mill yard and bridge. He had played the part over so many times in his head but tonight it looked perfect. His ultimate celluloid dream had arrived. This was to be the set for the film he would some day produce and direct. He could just make out the Deadwood stage coming down Tower Hill, with the steam rising off the team of four tired horses.

'Whooa ... there ... Fellahs. It's shure a pouring down tonight. Godamn Apache scout trailed us from Lorrha. Took a shot at him at Redwood but the varmint got away. Ain't going back out there tonight ...'

Then from directly behind, he heard a familiar gravelly tone;

'Well, ya know ... a man oughta do what he thinks is right.'

There could be no mistake this time. It had to be. It could only be ... The Duke

John Wayne himself, loading his Winchester rifle with that faraway look in his eye that spelt trouble. Time to get going!

The Final Curtain

Quackser made it into the show, just as the staff were putting away the night's takings in the box office. They were not showing much interest, so he got in for free. The cinema was nearly empty as he joined his pals in the dark humid interior. The film was a thriller called ***Key Largo***, which was interesting and absorbing initially but doggedly slow moving. Humphrey Bogart, an army veteran, had arrived at a small family hotel on the quays in Florida. It was off-season, so the only other guests were Edward G. Robinson and his assorted bunch of heavies. Lauren Bacall, the proprietor's daughter provided the love interest. The mobsters were supposedly going on a fishing trip. But one glance at this crew and you knew none of them ever coiled a loop or set a night-line. It seemed more likely were waiting on more of their ilk for some sort of underworld convention. The tension was palpable between the parties and the claustrophobia on screen was mirrored in the sticky conditions in the hall. Then came the mother of all tropical thunderstorms, near to hurricane force. Lauren Bacall foolishly upped the ante considerably, by spitting in the eye of gang boss Johnny Rocca (Edward G. Robinson) and the audience thought all hell was going to break loose. But it didn't. The plot sagged. In a bizarre sequence, a bunch of Indians appear (in Florida?) and the film itself went West after that interlude. It meandered on for another yawn inducing hour and for the bored young audience, THE END could not come half quick enough.

Outside, the storm had abated and the heavy rainfall had cleared the air as the small group left the cinema. What remained of the little gang made their separate ways home quietly along damp streets. They had sat through the show without being in any way conscious that they were part of an era that was coming to its end. Yes, television had arrived in a big way and within a few short years almost every home would have one shimmering in the living room corner. And there were to be plenty of other diversions on the way. Along with a gnawing sense that life was elsewhere, the Stella kids were now coming into their teens and words like the: Tech ... a trade ... pints ... girls ... boys ... Dublin ... London ... New York', were beginning to creep into their vocabulary. The whole world was out there beckoning in so many ways that did not include the old cinema. The world they had grown up in would soon be as far distant as the old West. Just like in the film **Brigadoon** once you leave home, you never really find it again.

Unlike George Baily (James Stuart) in **It's a Wonderful Life**, the local kids were not all destined to spend the remainder of their lives at home in their own insular Bedford Falls, much as they loved it. For a myriad of reasons, they were ready to move on in droves to the mean streets of larger, faster and more unforgiving societies. The Stella would soon become a place of the past. Good memories certainly but ultimately those of yesterday. There would be no turning back the clock. They knew there would be no last-reel comeback. They had now graduated from the pictures and were ready explore other worlds and there was a sense now that life was elsewhere.

When the cinema finally closed there was neither surprise nor regret amongst the local young people. The world was spinning and changing faster than anyone could have imagined. Many were already gone to the next phase of their lives and some had left the town for good. The films they had loved would recur only in dull reruns on the shrunken canvas of television on wet Sunday afternoons, devoid of their magic as blandly as if they had been microwaved. The world had changed and the feeling was that the Stella had fulfilled its task extremely well. A generation of boys and girls had grown up with it, been provided with hours of spectacle and entertainment in an atmosphere of fun, community and, friendship. This was the local *Cinema Paradiso*, bridging that invisible frontier between the mundane and the magical, a haven of nostalgia, imagination and escape from the claustrophobic confines of small town Ireland of the 50s and 60s. In testimony to the memory of a great little cinema, on behalf of all of the Stella kids everywhere;

Thanks for the memories